RACIAL
HEALING

*Equal Partners
Equal Responsibility*

Confronting the Fear
Between
Blacks and Whites

ANCHOR BOOKS
A Division of
Random House, Inc.
New York

RACIAL
HEALING

Harlon L. Dalton

First Anchor Books Edition, October 1996

Copyright © 1995 by Harlan L. Dalton

The Library of Congress has cataloged the Doubleday hardcover edition as follows:

Dalton, Harlon L.
Racial healing : confronting the fear between Blacks and Whites / Harlon L. Dalton. — 1st ed.
p.   cm.
1. United States—Race relations.   2. Intercultural communication—United States.   I. Title.
E185.615.D35   1995
305.8′00973—dc20   95-18882
CIP

ISBN 0-385-47517-9

www.anchorbooks.com

Printed in the United States of America
10   9   8

To Jill M. Strawn

Acknowledgments

First and foremost, I'd like to thank my brilliant and intrepid band of research assistants: Margareth Etienne, Rachel Hershfang, and Cecillia Wang, who were there at the beginning and integral to the entire creative process; Jane Park, who talked me through the tricky middle passage; and Betty Hung, without whom I never would have finished.

I'd also like to thank Lani Guinier, without whom I never would have started. Her disappointment by President Clinton made plain how difficult it is for Americans to deal openly and honestly with one another when it comes to race. More personally, Lani's by-the-hand guidance made it possible for me to do my part in promoting a frank, if occasionally painful, national conversation about race. Among other things, she introduced me to Charlotte Sheedy, a gifted literary agent with a flair for life and a powerful sense of justice. Charlotte, in turn, introduced me to Bill Thomas, who kept me going by believing in me, and who worked his editorial magic by infiltrating my brain.

Thanks also to David Golub and Kathryn Emmett, who in late-night conversation after conversation convinced me that I had an important contribution to make (albeit not the one we thought); to Ken and Renee Rocklin, who helped me free up the necessary emotional space; to Taunya Banks and Angela Harris for helping me find my voice; and to Stephen Sarfaty for productively confusing his obsession with mine.

I am exceedingly grateful to Jill Strawn for her wise counsel and unflagging support; to Valerie Dalton for help with family history and for modeling (via E-mail) how to dig deep and put oneself on the line; and to Louise Dalton and Ginny Berlenbach for being there in small ways as well as large.

Finally, I owe my authorial life to Matt Laskowski, beach bum and techno-nerd extraordinaire, who through creativity and sheer determination wrested six months' worth of literary ravings from my virus-decimated hard drive. Equally important, he managed to utter the words "You mean you don't have a backup or hard copy?" without a hint of condemnation or condescension.

Contents

RACIAL
HEALING

Introduction

We are loath to confront one another around race. We are afraid of tapping into pent-up anger, frustration, resentment, and pain. Even when we are not aware of harboring such feelings ourselves, we recognize that they exist in others. Our natural tendency is to hold them in check, in hopes that they will somehow fade away. Unfortunately, they will not. Tangled emotions and inexplicable behavior are the inevitable by-products of our nation's unresolved racial past. Until we deal with them, we resemble peasant villagers who continue to build on the slopes of an ancient but active volcano. Or, more precisely, we are like the mountain itself: oblivious to the gurgling deep within, proud of the new life it has nurtured, and hoping against hope that history will not repeat itself.

America's sorry racial state of affairs is also like a deep and abiding wound.[1] If left untreated, it will continue to ooze and fester. Too often we act as if we are mesmerized by some collective mother who keeps whispering, "Leave it alone. Don't pick the scab." But the truth is that unless we periodically clean out the wound, clear it of accumulated debris, allow it to breathe, and apply sterile dressings, we will never be able to heal and move on. And even then, we must remain attentive to the ever present possibility of infection.

We have run away from race for far too long. We are so afraid of inflaming the wound that we fail to deal with what remains America's central social problem. We will never achieve racial healing if we do not confront each other, take risks, make ourselves vulnerable, put pride aside, say all the things we are not supposed to say in mixed company—in short, put on the table all of our fears, trepidations, wishes, and hopes.

The first half of this book is intended to shepherd that process along. There are, of course, many real and powerful reasons why we shrink from engaging one another around issues of race. And even when we do try, our efforts often backfire, flame out, or turn to dust. But true engagement *is* possible, and I do my best to show how.

Of course, it will do us little good to heal our racial wounds if we are ultimately destined to inflict them anew. Yet that is inevitable so long as race and social power are intimately linked. Indeed, perpetuating racial hierarchy in a society that professes to be egalitarian is destructive of the spirit as well as of the body politic. But change will not come on its own. If we do not actively intervene, the existing pecking order will constantly reassert itself even as we work to overcome the errors of the past. Those near the bottom may reverse positions from time to time, but the basic structure will endure.

If we as a nation are to achieve *lasting* racial healing, we must thoroughly dismantle that structure. Simply removing formal impediments to equality is not enough; the pecking order thrives on hidden power and invisible rules. Nor would we gain much by maintaining the pecking order while changing who is on top. Our goal should be to transform how power and prestige are distributed in society and, ultimately, the very meaning of race itself.

But before we can truly imagine, let alone bring about such a transformation, we must first get our respective houses in order. We have to change how we think. We have to change how we act. We have to give up some of what we currently value, and begin valuing some of what we currently disdain. In the second half of the book, I try to mark the path.

In so doing, I confine myself to the work that Blacks and Whites must do, leaving for another day the specific challenges facing Asian-Americans, Native Americans, and Latinos. That is because I write mostly out of my own personal experience. As it is, for me to attempt to articulate the needs, concerns, strengths, and foibles of my own community is fairly presumptuous. To attempt more would be presumptuous in the extreme. I could, of course, rely heavily on the experiences of others, but that would lead to a very different kind of book.

I realize that there are many downsides to viewing a world of color through a lens that refracts only black and white. A major one is that the Black experience tends to become the template against which the experiences of *all* people of color are measured. Another is that frictions among people of color tend to be rendered invisible. I try to avoid both of these pitfalls.

The specific challenges facing Whites are different from those facing people of color. How could it be otherwise, given the distinct historical experiences and present circumstances of each race? The first step is for Whites to conceive of themselves as members of a race and to recognize the advantages that attach to simply having white skin. Many of my White friends readily embrace their ethnic identity, or define themselves by religion, geographic region, or profession. But few spontaneously think of themselves in racial terms. In part, that is because in settings where Whites dominate, being White is not noteworthy. It is like the tick of a familiar clock, part of the easily tuned-out background noise.

The same is true of other facets of identity. Dominance makes the difference. For example, straight people ordinarily do not define themselves in terms of their sexual orientation or think of it as playing much of a role in how their lives unfold. But place them in a predominantly gay setting, and they become acutely aware of their heterosexuality. Similarly, a working-class Irish Catholic accustomed to thinking of himself in ethnic rather than racial terms would most likely feel whiter than white while walking along 125th Street in Harlem.

The challenge for White folk is to realize, even when they are not in the minority, that *their* race matters too. It establishes their place in the social pecking order. It hangs over the relationships they establish with people of color. Like it or not, their unchosen racial identity has a profound influence on their life prospects. Like it or not, their fate as individuals is tied in complex ways to the fate of Whites as a whole.

We have long since grown accustomed to thinking of Blacks as being "racially disadvantaged." Rarely, however, do we refer to Whites as "racially *ad*vantaged," even though that is an equally apt characterization of the existing inequality. "Membership," as the folk from American Express remind us, "has its privileges." Whites move to the head of the line simply by being born White.

Many of my White friends blanch at this idea. It makes them deeply uncomfortable. It makes them feel complicitous in something over which they have little personal control. It leaves them feeling somehow guilty while providing no ready way to discharge the guilt. And, frankly, it raises the uncomfortable question of whether they ought to give up something, hand something back, surrender the fruits of their privilege. But even though acknowledging White skin privilege is difficult, awkward, and discomfiting, real progress depends on it. For to ignore the reality of race-based privilege is to deny the very meaning of race in our society. True, our ultimate goal should be to transform that meaning, but we can't get there without starting where we are.

The second step toward racial progress is for White folk to accept partial ownership of America's race problem. Most Whites, according to polls, do not view the current racial malaise as their responsibility.[2] One need only tune in to talk show radio to get the message. "I didn't create the mess, and I'm not in a position to clean it up. I'm willing to pitch in if others do their part, but if you ask me, Blacks seem to be their own worst enemies."

While this attitude is understandable, it is altogether wrongheaded. No human being living or dead, Black, White, or indifferent, created the entire mess, but many of us (myself included) have added to it or helped to perpetuate it in one way or another. If we were entirely honest with ourselves, we'd see there is probably onus enough for everybody. As for the suggestion that the Black community has somehow forfeited its right to sympathy and support by virtue of its own self-destructive behavior, the proposition's self-vindicating flavor should give us pause. Besides, unless one attributes the community's self-inflicted wounds to some character defect inherent in the race, we cannot simply dismiss the lively possibility that White indifference and "benign neglect"[3] have contributed to the problem.

Questions of responsibility to the side, we must all pitch in to remedy America's racial ills. After all, our fates are inextricably linked. Unless we are prepared to abandon America's great cities, it is in everyone's self-interest to improve the lot of Black urban dwellers. Unless we are willing to accept an economy that operates on fewer than all of its cylinders, we have an interest in ensuring that people of every hue develop and utilize their talents and skills. Unless Whites don't mind being forced to choose between paying for skyrocketing social services and tolerating squalor in the midst of plenty, they have a stake in change. Of course, the costs imposed by racial disharmony are more than economic. All of us are losers to the extent that we miss out on the opportunity to interact with, learn from and be inspired by folk who grew up on the other side of the color line.

I suspect that many White folk shy away from owning America's race problem because they recognize that it is a steady source of discomfort, anxiety, and uncertainty. Many suffer from race weariness as it is. They fear that the struggle is never-ending, and are of the view that nothing we have tried to date has worked. Unfortunately, there are no guarantees. We are trying to climb out of a hole that we spent three hundred years digging. But I have to believe that by focusing on the problem together, as equal partners with equal responsibility, we can harness the wit, the will, and the energy to create a new day.

Blacks face different challenges. Our first order of business is to rethink and retell who we are and how racism has affected our lives. There is a stock story that we tend to trot out when the occasion demands, but it is badly out of date. It fails to take account of the many twists and turns in our fate since slavery. It does not acknowledge the great variety within our own community along virtually every dimension—class, color, racial consciousness, life experiences, lifestyle, and livelihood. It fails to explain why some Blacks are doing quite well, even as so many others are doing poorly. It does not address the structural changes in the American and world economies that have tended to lock most of us into the places carved out by past segregation and discrimination. It does not address the changes in our own culture that have hampered our progress and contributed to our feelings of hopelessness and despair.

Because the story we tell about ourselves leaves so much to be desired, we are no longer able to make White America "feel" for us. Worse, in our heart of hearts we don't find the story convincing either, which leaves us feeling truly victimized yet unable to pinpoint why. That way lies madness and despair.

Meanwhile, as we stick to the old party line many Whites and some neoconservative Blacks are retelling our story for us. Their retelling is quite partial, and is limited to our warts with no mention at all of the frog who kissed us. It is even more simplistic than the tired story we tell, but it has the virtue of relative freshness and does contain elements of truth. We therefore need to retell our story in all its complexity. Only then will we be in a position to respond convincingly to the many misgivings that rob us of sympathy and support. We can't very well reframe the debate if we are intent on ducking half of it.

We also need to pull together as a community. We no longer have a sense of common purpose. We lack a set of common aspirations. We are increasingly disconnected from one another—socially, culturally, economically, and geographically. And we have even begun to fear one another. Under the circumstances, we are in a poor position from which to urge the nation to mend its racial ways.

Historically, the Black community has been bound together by a sense of shared oppression, a common political vision, a common culture, and common social institutions. Given the partial disintegration of each of these ties, our second challenge is to thoroughly rethink what, if anything, Black people have in common as we approach the millennium. Perhaps some of the old bonds can be strengthened. Perhaps there are others that we have overlooked.

As we set about the business of reimagining community, we should embrace our differences rather than squelch them, and pay honor to the richness and complexity of the Black experience. Our diversity is an asset, not a hindrance. We must also find new and different ways for people to contribute to and feel connected with one another. It is important, for example, to remember that geography needn't be destiny. The fact that folk are now able to flee the "hood" once they have made it does not necessarily mean that their ability or willingness to contribute to inner-city life is at an end. Family is family. The trick is to figure out how to maintain a sense of kinship that transcends space and time.

The third challenge facing Black America is cultural. It is imperative that we take stock of the values, customs, modes of artistic expression, institutions, and social practices that bear our imprint. After all, any serious attempt to engage White America in a conversation about racial justice will eventually come around to some rather probing questions about how we live our lives. Indeed, that part of the conversation has already started—without our participation.

It has become virtually an article of faith among many Whites that the problems of Black America are of our own making and stem from what are often termed pathologies in our culture. Such sentiments are by no means limited to the Rush Limbaughs of the world. In fact, White friends tell me that this viewpoint is widespread even among liberal caring folk.

Despite my suspicions regarding what motivates people to embrace this "defective culture" thesis, and my fear that any acknowledgment by us of cultural weakness will be thrown in our faces, I am convinced that we cannot afford to ignore it or give it the back of our hand. We have no choice but to enter into and reframe the debate regarding our culture. If others are perverting the conversation to serve their own ends, we must call them on it, but we cannot continue to let them carry the day through our silence. We must, I am afraid, defy those elders who counsel that dirty linen should not be washed in public. There are, after all, very few private places left.

But first we must decide what we are about. How *do* we see our culture? What do we have to offer that is truly unique? Which of our values, styles, and distinctive modes of behavior has special meaning for us? Which aspects of the culture attributed to us are merely mainstream values run amok? We need not preserve and defend everything we do. We can, for example, choose whether or not to defend the 2 Live Crew's misogyny. We don't have to insist that babies having babies is a desirable cultural practice in the Black community.

All of us, Black and White, must work toward a new way of coexisting, of sharing power, and of ensuring that anatomy is not destiny. I can't say for sure what a racially just America would look like, but if we ever gave it much thought, we might discover that we are more united in what we desire for the future than in how we deal with the present. If so, we ought to consider working backward. By spending a little time dreaming together about the promised land, we just might figure out how to bring it about.

PART ONE

A Strange Encounter

About a decade ago, I decided to move a little closer to the center of town. I hadn't been in New Haven long, and was still sorting out where and how I wanted to live.

Money was not much of an issue. As a law professor, I am rather well paid, especially in relation to New Haven's depressed real estate market. Moreover, I was unattached, had few debts or other obligations, and had a fairly simple lifestyle. But unconstrained choices are often the hardest to make. They force us to decide what we are really about. They oblige us to confront, or at least acknowledge, the various selves that dwell within us.

I like neighborhoods that are true neighborhoods, places where you feel connected to the folk down the block, psychically as well as physically. At the same time, I value my privacy, and often prefer solitude to engagement, anonymity to community. I love cities and streets and the clamor they breed. But I also love songbirds and trees and crickets and peepers. I like to live close enough to work so that I scarcely notice the commute, yet far enough away to really feel away. Finally, I prefer to live in neighborhoods where people come in all flavors, and sleep better at night knowing that other Black folk are near at hand.

With surprisingly little effort, I found a house that seemed to suit me fine. It didn't meet all my needs, of course, but I had little trouble imagining myself living there and thriving. The park across the street and the hill out back were the clinchers.

In due course, I packed up my belongings and engaged the services of a professional mover. I had no choice, having exploited my friends' strong backs just nine months earlier. However, not knowing how careful "The Man With a Van" would be or whether he was adequately insured, I saved a lot of the fragile stuff to move myself.

After more round trips than I care to remember, I grabbed my plants, apologized to the house for being so fickle, and turned the key for the last time. As I readied myself to drive off for good, I heard someone gently tapping on my car window. I looked up and saw a youngish-looking woman peering into the car and smiling quizzically.

Instantaneously, several facts about her registered in my brain: she was female, White, roughly my age, and a stranger. And there was one thing more. She did not seem the least bit apprehensive about accosting a strange man, and a Black one to boot. "How odd," I thought.

I rolled down the window, reflexively removed my sunglasses so as to appear less forbidding, and said something brilliant, like "Hi." She responded in kind; then, scarcely pausing to breathe, she asked, "Why are you moving?" I was taken aback by her boldness. Who was she, and what right did she have to get into my personal business? Surely I did not owe this complete stranger an explanation of my comings and goings.

Despite my misgivings, I found myself fumbling for an answer. The complete truth was much too complex, so I settled for a socially acceptable piece of it. I then attempted to turn the tables. "Who are you," I asked. My friendly assailant smiled brightly and said, "I am Jadwiga Sutak. I live across the street." I couldn't help but notice that she spoke with a pronounced movie-familiar accent. "Where are you from?" I asked. "Poland. I have been here for six months."

I told her my name and then, somewhat sheepishly, requested that she repeat hers. "How do you spell it?" I asked, as I tried to burn the unfamiliar syllables into my brain. "You may call me Judy if you like." "Which do *you* prefer?" I asked. Sidestepping the question, she explained that her co-workers had concluded that "Jadwiga" was too difficult to pronounce, and had therefore rechristened her "Judy." As someone whose own name is sometimes considered a mouthful, I assured her that I would go with "Jadwiga."

Jadwiga then barraged me with a series of questions that made the first one seem like mashed potatoes. She quickly zeroed in on race. "When I pass by the welfare office on my way to work, how come all I see is you people standing in line? I hardly ever see White people. Why is it just you people?" Whoa!!! That loaded phrase—"you people"—rattled around in my brain. Instantly, I envisioned a gaggle of Black folk in bib overalls, chicken bones piled high all around, waiting for a handout. Was this woman racist or what? She then continued to push my buttons. "At the high school where I take English-as-a-second-language classes, I can't concentrate because the Black kids keep running up and down the halls yelling and making a lot of noise. Why do they do that?"

I stared at her hard, and tried to decide whether to wither her with scorn or ice her with contempt. "Damn," I thought, "why did I remove my sunglasses?" But as I silently debated my options, I couldn't help noticing that the face staring back at me was gentle and inquisitive. It radiated intelligence, warmth, and genuine curiosity. Despite the fact that I was on red alert, I realized that Jadwiga Sutak had come in peace. She meant me, and my people, no harm.

The loaded phrases and images had no special meaning for her, and she had no idea that they would produce near-apoplexy in me. She was simply trying to account for what she had seen and heard. She had stepped into a cultural cow pie without even knowing it. It was as if she had just dropped in from the moon. And in a sense, she had. Not literally, of course, but at that moment Poland and the moon seemed equally far away. With homegrown White folk, I could simply assume that they "knew better" and were just trying to get my goat. But this alien inquisitor was clearly different.

So I tried to answer Jadwiga's question, and the many others that crowded in after it. My first impulse was to be facile. After all, I had developed a fairly decent soft-shoe which usually enabled me to "get over" in racial conversations without investing much energy or emotion. Unfortunately, Jadwiga wasn't impressed. Apparently, she did not realize that she should be grateful that I had even deigned to respond. No one had told her that conversations about race are supposed to just skim the surface.

Once I realized that Jadwiga wasn't going to be easily put off, I tried to meet her questions head-on. I soon discovered that I had no easy answers to give, in part because we couldn't just begin the conversation in the here and now. We had to go back, to fill in, to put things in some kind of context. That proved especially difficult, because Jadwiga and I had no common history, no shared frame of reference, no common culture.

I went back to the beginning. I spoke with feeling, and a bit too much drama, about how my people had been snatched out of Africa, placed on slave ships, and brought to these shores in chains. I paid tribute to the millions who died in the middle passage. I tried to capture the horrors of slavery, and the toll it took on individuals, families, and the institutions that bound them together. Jadwiga listened thoughtfully, reflected for a moment, and then asked, gently, "But wasn't that a long time ago?"

"Not really," I said. I then related to her stories my father told me. He often spoke wistfully of childhood afternoons spent listening to his grandmother describe firsthand what life had been like during slavery. He didn't seem to remember the details, and was resistant to my prodding, but Daddy clearly took comfort in having seen fleshly proof that our family had triumphed over pure evil. He loved to describe my great-grandmother. She was a familiar-looking old woman, toothless and proud, sitting at the kitchen table with a Bible clutched in her hand. She could not read, of course, but the Good Book was her solace, and she quoted from it often.

Jadwiga listened, and seemed genuinely moved. But she still was not satisfied. "What does that have to do with the

way kids behave today?" she asked. Her doggedness caught
me off guard. Pressing the slavery button at least should have
bought me a little breathing space. In my experience, White
people could be counted on to express at length their keen
embarrassment and regret about the institution of slavery. But
not Jadwiga. Sure, slavery must have been awful, but it wasn't
her fault. She had only been in this country for six months.

It was clearly time to flash forward. I tried to illustrate
how the legacy of slavery endured long after its formal end. I
talked about Black Codes, Jim Crow laws, segregation, and
discrimination. And I made it personal. I described the acute
embarrassment I felt as a child when, while driving cross-
country in the late 1950s, my family had to choose between
sleeping in the car and searching for the local "Colored town"
because the motels on the Interstate always seemed to have
just run out of rooms. "But," said Jadwiga, "you don't have to
do that anymore, do you?" "No, I guess not."

Frustrated and dazed, I realized that something more
was needed. Although tracing historical antecedents was
surely important, somehow I needed to connect them to the
here and now. It is easy enough to assert that one or another
current difficulty is the legacy of slavery. It is far more difficult to show precisely where and how past and present meet.
Often the connections exist in the shadowy world of attitudes,
assumptions, expectations, and perspective. How could I possibly capture all that? Maybe if I had a week or two . . .

I sneaked a peek at my watch. To my surprise, Jadwiga
and I already had been talking for an hour and a half, with me
sitting inside the car and her leaning against it. Somehow it
hadn't seemed right to invite her in. After all, we were strang-

ers. I guess I could have gotten out of the car, but by the time I realized that I was in for an extended conversation, the setting had ceased to seem awkward. Also, I probably liked feeling that I was in the driver's seat, particularly since virtually nothing else about the conversation supported that conclusion.

As I looked up, Jadwiga read my face perfectly. "You have to go, don't you?" I nodded. She smiled. I thought about trying to put into words how special the afternoon had been, but realized that I could not. At least not without running into the very same cultural barrier that had made our entire encounter so frustrating and at the same time so exhilarating. Jadwiga and I expressed mutual regret that the conversation had to come to an end, and vowed to pick it up again in the near future. After an exchange of telephone numbers and mutual assurances that it was really O.K. to call, I bid her and my old neighborhood goodbye.

Jadwiga and I did stay in touch. In fact, we formed a fine friendship that lasted until she moved out of state a couple of years later. Our conversations continued to be lively, unblinkered, and joyfully frank. Somehow, though, we never really got into it about race again. We were certainly attentive to the racial dimension of whatever we happened to be discussing, but we never again took on race as a topic du jour. There were so many other things to talk about: geopolitics; political theory and practice; Polish culture and society; the American scene as seen through Jadwiga's eyes. And sometimes we just hung out.

I often think back to that first serendipitous meeting. It was, for me, a one-of-a-kind experience. It's not as though I

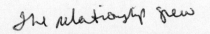
The relationship grew

haven't had my share of "race conversations" in my twoscore and seven. In fact, because I cross racial boundaries every day and am a generally genial sort, I often am asked to serve as sort of a spokesmodel for Black America. Nevertheless, my initial encounter with Jadwiga was truly unique.

Most cross-racial conversations about race fall into a particular pattern. The typical conversation resembles nothing so much as a hastily thrown-together press conference, with Whites cast as small-town journalists and Blacks in the role of visiting potentates from some obscure foreign country. The questions are pro forma and polite; the answers guarded and general. The participants stick to the tried-and-true, the urge to make news being more than offset by the desire not to cause an international incident. The journalist asks, "How long will you be staying in the United States?" when what she really means is: "How can your dirt-poor country afford to send you gallivanting around the world?" The foreign leader resists the temptation to say what's really on his mind ("If the rest of your country is anything like this two-bit burg, I can't wait to go home") and instead responds gravely, "Only as long as is necessary to awaken the conscience of this great nation to the plight of my people."

Whenever the conversation turns to race, precious little gets said that hasn't already been thoroughly canvassed in previous conversations. Without giving it much thought, we know which topics are safe and how far to push. To be sure, the rules of engagement—and nonengagement—are complex. Black folk, for example, can tease Whites about lying out in the sun in order to look like us, but White folk cannot tease Blacks about straightening our hair. Even so, most of the time we know where the boundaries are.

Propriety reigns; tension and acrimony are forbidden. Attempts to press beyond the commonly accepted limits are preceded by a kind of ritualized permission seeking. "I hope you don't find this offensive, but . . ." Frequently we chastise ourselves. "Why did I ask that? I sound like a complete idiot. What's he gonna say, 'Yes, I am deeply offended, but let's talk anyway'?" And on the other side: "Is she implying that I am overly sensitive? What a great way to silence me. If I challenge her it just proves her point. Then again, perhaps I am a *little* hypersensitive." Thus, before the conversation even begins, the seeds of its undoing are sown.

Somehow, Jadwiga and I managed to get beyond all that. Our conversation was freewheeling, uninhibited, and robust. When we generated heat, we didn't mistake it for the fire next time. We did not confuse the rituals of respect for respect itself. We were able to hear one another, to push one another, to be honest with one another, to engage one another.

PART TWO

Healing the Past/
Transforming the Present

ENGAGEMENT

Engagement is critical to healing. It has the potential to transform our lives. It can change the way we see, hear, think, and feel. It can propel us across vast differences in culture and experience. It can move us past our fears. When we engage, truly engage, we let go and grab on at the same time. We loose our hold on old truths even as we reach out for new ones. We sacrifice neatness for the messiness of reality and comfort for the occasional pain of honest dealing.

In focusing so heavily on seeing, hearing, thinking, and feeling, I run the risk of seeming indifferent to the need for *action* to address America's festering social problems. What, for example, does all this blather have to do with the daunting task of reversing the downward spiral of our inner cities? What hard choices are we going to make *today* regarding, say, funding for drug treatment programs, or the provision of health care to the children of undocumented workers?

My answer, in brief, is that at this particular moment in American history, meaningful action at the societal level is virtually impossible. As a nation we lack a consensus concerning how to deal with the problems that bedevil us most. We seem unable to take sustained action in any direction for very long. And we don't trust anyone enough to let them lead. We are, in short, politically paralyzed.

The reasons for this paralysis are several, but chief among them is our failure to engage each other openly and honestly around race. Think about the issues that sit atop the American agenda: crime; welfare reform; taxes; government spending; the plight of the middle class; family values; immigration; drug abuse; AIDS. Together they carry enough racial freight to sink a nation.

In the popular imagination, criminals are Black or Brown; crime victims White. Welfare cheats are dark of hue; the "forgotten middle class" is light. Governmental "taxing and spending" favors racial minorities and comes out of the hides of the White majority. Problem immigrants have yellow or brown skin; the citizens who foot the bill do not. Needless to say, I do not endorse these beliefs, or the skewed view of reality they project. My point is simply that our thinking about the nation's most pressing social problems has become deeply "racialized"—saturated with attitudes, beliefs, and fears about race.

We tend to dance around this fact whenever we publicly debate social policy. In our zeal to approach issues in a "color-blind" fashion, we often push their complex and volatile racial dimensions underground. When we do so, we of course make it virtually impossible to frame policies that thoughtfully take race into account. Less obviously, burying race makes it difficult to formulate sensible "race-neutral" social policy as well, for we cannot escape the powerful sensation that something is amiss and that somehow the game is not being played straight. If, instead, we were to surface our racial misgivings and candidly explore the ways in which they influence our policy preferences, we just might get unstuck. We would spend a lot less time searching for double meanings and hidden agendas, and would be much less likely to miscalculate each other's intentions. And we would be in a much better position to design and pursue win-win solutions.

In retrospect, it was relatively easy for Jadwiga and me to engage one another, largely because we were total strangers. Not only had we not met before; I had never met anyone quite like her. The fact that we lacked a common history and culture meant that we could not fall into the trap of relying on stored-up assumptions about each other. We had to communicate in complete sentences and to keep checking to see if we were on the same page. Moreover, the fact that we had no "past" meant that we had very little baggage to shed. Although we had no particular reason to trust one another, we had no deep-seated reasons to distrust.

On the other hand, while my engagement with Jadwiga was certainly rewarding, even greater rewards await those of us who grew up on opposite sides of the same historical street. For our common history binds us just as surely as it divides us. Our roots are inextricably intertwined. The fact that we have met so many times before, figuratively if not literally, means that we have much to contribute to each other's salvation. We have much to learn and unlearn, and many wounds to heal, but we have even more to lose if we do not.

How do we start, we who share a history? Thinking back

my encounter with Jadwiga, I realize that it is full of useful lessons. *Something* made the two of us connect. Doubtless temperament and personality played a part. I was clearly taken with Jadwiga's boldness, her indifference to convention, and her infectious curiosity, and felt that I would look like a wuss if I did not respond in kind. But personal chemistry does not begin to explain why we decided to listen to each other, to take risks, and to put everything on the table.

Six additional factors stand out. First off, Jadwiga was willing to take the initiative. She was not afraid of me in spite of all the scary baggage this society attaches to Black men. It did not occur to her that I might dislike her just because of her skin color, and I soon realized that she did not dislike me because of mine.

Second, Jadwiga did not presume she already knew everything about me that mattered. She did not repair to a storehouse of presumptions and expectations to figure out who I was and what made me tick. She wanted to *learn* about me and my people, as distinct from merely confirming (or even disconfirming) what she already knew. As the conversation stretched on, I came to realize that there was much about her that I didn't know.

Third, Jadwiga wanted to hear about me from my own mouth. She didn't seek a more "objective" source—i.e., another White person. In truth, she had already heard a great deal about Black people from her White co-workers, but she wanted to check it out with me. She did not accept their version of reality simply because she shared their skin color.

Fourth, Jadwiga approached me as an individual *and* as a Black man. She made it quite plain that her curiosity extended both to me as me ("Why are you moving?") and to me as the embodiment of my race ("How come you people . . . ?"). She did not pretend to be color-blind. At the same time, she never reduced me to my race.

Fifth, Jadwiga truly listened to what I had to say. I didn't have to worry that my words were being filtered through the screen of her own fears and misgivings. She wasn't listening to see if she would be blamed or exonerated or called to account. She just listened.

Finally, Jadwiga responded as well as listened. She was willing to tell me what she honestly thought. She did not worry overly much about offending me, and she did not take offense no matter how heated or pointed my comments were.

I focus on the qualities Jadwiga brought to the table because it was she who made the conversation happen. I had not the slightest interest in getting drawn into anything real, and was sorely tempted to dip into my usual bag of diversionary tactics. But Jadwiga's incredible openness and her thoughtful persistence made me want to hang in there, at least for a while.

As I think back over what made Jadwiga and me connect, it is small wonder that true engagement is so rare. Usually, no one wants to take the initiative. Talking honestly about race feels risky. We aren't quite sure how to do it or where it will lead. The upside is uncertain and largely unknown. Even if things go well, what will be accomplished? The downside, however, feels much more predictable. Although we may not be able to say precisely how, we tend to believe that if things go badly there will be hell to pay.

White folk often hesitate to dive into the subject of race

out of fear that they will make a mistake, say something
stupid, display insensitivity, or, worst of all, come across as
racist. Such fears can lead to elaborate minuets. For example,
last year I bumped into a student in the parking lot. As Kris
and I stood there catching up on the latest, we were joined by
one of her other professors. The three of us chatted amiably,
each, I suspect, taking secret pride in our ability to communicate comfortably and easily across three generations. Unfortunately, things soon came unstuck.

Joe (my colleague) mentioned to Kris that he had finally
gotten a chance to read through and comment upon the term
paper she had submitted to him. She could pick it up anytime
that was convenient. Kris, who is Black, thanked him, but
then asked whether he was sure he meant to be speaking to
her rather than her roommate, who had also written a paper
for the same course. "I just ask because lots of people mix us
up," she explained, "including close friends." Joe looked
crestfallen. "I'm pretty sure it's yours," he said, or words to
that effect, and then beat a hasty retreat.

Realizing how awkward the scene had been, Kris sought
to assure me that she hadn't meant to embarrass my colleague
or to suggest that he had difficulty telling Black people apart.
She and her roommate had been mistaken for each other so
often that she had just gotten into the habit of anticipating
confusion. She also sought to assure me that she thought the
world of Professor Goldstein, and viewed him as one of the
most fair-minded and socially aware people she knew. I told
Kris I would convey her sentiments to him if the opportunity
presented itself, and observed that I knew from personal experience that Professor Goldstein "has our back."

A couple of days later, I ran into Joe in the hallway. Before I could get a word in edgewise, he said he hoped I hadn't drawn any negative conclusions about him from the parking-lot conversation. He had, he assured me, gone back and checked, and the paper in question was indeed the one written by Kris. I responded that even if he had mixed up two Black people, I couldn't care less. He was someone who had taken me seriously even when I was a law student. He had taken the time to truly get to know me, and over the years had made it quite plain that he accepted me in all my complexity. He had welcomed me into his home. He had paid me the compliment of arguing with me when he thought I was wrong, and of taking seriously my challenges to him even when they involved issues (Israeli politics, for example) in which he was invested emotionally. How could I ever think of him as racially insensitive or uncaring? Joe looked appreciative, but I am not sure he was ever fully convinced that the racial minefields between us had long since been swept away.

Sometimes Whites fail to take the initiative in matters of race out of the misguided belief that they have little of value to say. They routinely defer to people of color, and are reluctant even to broach the subject without a clear signal that it is O.K. to do so.

This inhibition is felt even by folk who think about race a lot. Rachel Hershfang, who is White, served as one of my research assistants. During an interview for a summer job at a law firm, she was asked about the line on her résumé that said "helps Professor with preparation of book on race in America." She responded eagerly, outlining the book's major themes, describing some of her more interesting assignments, and sharing some of the insights she had gained in the course of her work. She also spoke animatedly about the joys of working as part of a multiracial research team, alongside Cecilia Wang, who is Chinese-American, and Margareth Etienne, who is an African-American of Haitian descent.

The interviewer seemed truly impressed, and volunteered that she too had participated in efforts to foster racial understanding. As she related the details, Rachel listened intently, grateful to find a fellow traveler in such an unlikely place. Then suddenly a frightening possibility popped into her head. The well-tanned interviewer with the curly hair and light brown eyes—could she be Black? Trying not to panic, Rachel scanned the woman's features for clues. "Damn," she thought, "I can't tell." She hurriedly replayed the entire conversation in her mind. Had she said anything offensive? Had she said anything stupid? Had she been presumptuous? The conversation had been fine so long as she thought she was talking to someone White, but did she have the right to say the same things to a Black woman?

Sometimes White folk avoid talking about race in order to respect the presumed needs of people of color who seem weary of the subject. I must confess that I have taken advantage of this tendency by, on occasion, looking just pained enough to discourage a conversation from flowering. Similarly, Whites who are close to people of color sometimes skirt around race so as not to impose a strain on the relationship— kind of like not wanting to risk spoiling a good friendship by introducing romance. Ironically, people of color often interpret such reticence as evidence of their White friends' disinterest in truly getting to know them. Finally, White people sometimes hold back because they are afraid of tapping into resentment and anger, and of being presented with what feels like an overwhelming set of demands.

People of color, on the other hand, often bite their tongues out of fear that if they bring up race they will be seen as "troublemakers" or "agitators" bent on fomenting "racial unrest."[1] We know from long experience that such labels are often used to keep us in check, and to justify dismissing whatever we have to say, no matter how worthy. We fear that even if our words are heard, our ideas will be subtly devalued and disrespected. At best we will be humored, treated indulgently, or handled with kid gloves. We also worry that if we own up to the problems that beset our communities—the high incidence of HIV in Black and Latino communities, for example, or of alcoholism among Native Americans who live on reservations—our words will somehow be turned against us. They will be taken as evidence of our racial inferiority rather than of our historic subordination.

We, all of us, need to overcome, or at least transcend, these fears. Some of them grow out of a belief that we don't know enough to avoid embarrassing ourselves. But the great thing about ignorance is that it can always be cured through learning. More often, our fears stem from the belief that there is little margin for error in race conversations, and that the relationship between us and whomever we would engage is not strong enough or resilient enough to withstand pressure. However, in this respect human relationships (whether professional or personal, casual or ongoing) are like the human body. They can be strengthened through regular exercise and made more resilient by frequent stretching. There may be a bit of next-day soreness, but the improved capacity, not to mention the feeling of virtue, makes it all worthwhile. Similarly, the best answer to our fear of being put down, devalued, and not heard is more engagement. To do otherwise is to collaborate in our own denigration. And although silence may ensure that our own words will not be turned against us, it can do little to change the mind-sets that, if unchallenged, will continue to be our undoing.

There are, of course, reasons for retreating into silence that are not born of fear. For many of us people of color, there is a part of us that really doesn't want to let White America in on that which we regard as uniquely ours. This cultural isolationism finds public expression in T-shirts that proudly (if dismissively) proclaim: "It's a Black Thang. You wouldn't understand." The same sentiment, less bodaciously expressed, is felt across the rainbow. There is also a part of us that is tired of being the ones who do all the work, of bearing the burden of "educating White folk," as my people say. In this respect, we are rather like feminists (of every color) who insist that men share the responsibility for educating themselves about how gender oppression operates.

Finally, and perhaps most importantly, speaking out candidly and forthrightly about race poses certain psychological risks for people of color. When we truly commit ourselves to the conversation, we risk tapping into a storehouse of powerful feelings. Especially when we speak from the heart, we tap into anger and resentment that is difficult to modulate. We never know when we might just "go off," and sail way beyond the bounds of appropriate behavior. Worse, we never know when we might unleash corrosive feelings within ourselves that we need to keep in check, or at least in balance, as a matter of simple survival. Anger, out of control, eventually consumes its own host.

Of course, those same corrosive feelings can threaten our well-being even when they are bottled up. For that reason, we are probably better off erring on the side of speaking our minds, especially in settings where there is little risk of financial or other retribution. We should also resist the temptation to refuse to engage White folk (or other people of color, for that matter) out of resentment over cultural imperialism. The provocation is clear. Native Americans, for example, have countless reasons to resent the usurpation and appropriation of significant aspects of their culture. It can't be long before American Express begins sponsoring vision quest tours and the Sharper Image starts selling mail-order sweat lodges. Nevertheless, meaningful racial engagement is too rare for it to be boycotted. Far better to make our cultural concerns part of an ongoing dialogue.

Even when someone does get up the nerve to initiate race talk in mixed company, the ensuing conversation often founders because the assumptions we make about one another get in the way of real communication. It is, of course, perfectly natural to assume things about people. After all, when grappling with race, as with most aspects of social life, we have to rely on accumulated experience for guidance. We could not function otherwise. We could no more begin every day anew, as if we were seeing the world for the first time, than we could return to the womb.

When we look out over a duck pond and see a mallard, we recognize it not because of its inherent mallardness but because we have encountered mallards before. We have created a mallard category in our brains and have learned to distinguish its members from fish, airplanes, geese, and even other ducks. Each new mallard we meet confirms what we know about the others, adds to our store of information about the category, or causes us to reevaluate it. But whichever way we come out, we don't contemplate new mallards separate and apart from what we already know about their kind.

The same is true of human beings. So long as race is one of the categories we use to organize our experiences, we will of necessity view each new person of a particular kind against the backdrop of our prior experiences with others of that kind. Those past encounters need not be face to face. Much of what I know about mallards comes from what I have read, seen on television, or been told. But to the extent that I credit what I learn, it influences my expectations and assumptions. If, for example, I have read that mallards mate for life and am used to seeing mallards in pairs, I will tend to look for a nearby brown duck every time I spot one with the familiar green head. Similarly, if in my experience White people who encounter me on a darkened street often act as if they expect to be mugged, I will incorporate that knowledge in my dealings with White strangers.

One winter evening early on in my career as a law professor, I ventured out to my neighborhood ATM machine for my weekly cash fix. The weather was chilly, but fortunately the machine was housed inside a large glass cubicle. To gain entry, I inserted my bank card in a slot next to the door, waited for the buzz, and pulled on the handle.

I entered my password and checked my balance. Then, just as I was beginning to enter the amount I wished to withdraw, I heard a rattling noise behind me, as if someone was trying to force the door. I turned around and saw a casually dressed, slightly unkempt White man, about my size and age, flashing his ATM card and gesturing for me to let him in. Since I wasn't particularly interested in letting him see how much I was withdrawing, much less in letting him share my fortune, I shook my head and waved my hands in a way that was clearly meant to be discouraging.

To be honest, I really wasn't afraid of him. I had quickly sized him up and determined that he was no threat. In retrospect, that judgment was probably rooted in lessons I had learned as a teenager decades before. In the crowd I ran with, it was accepted wisdom that "whiteboys" are all "punks," meaning that you could always get the best of them, even if they were bigger or older. That was because they were afraid of us. "All you've got to do is look fierce and maybe act a little crazy," I had been sagely counseled. (The Italians who lived on the north side of town constituted an exception to this rule. They, reportedly, were fearless and "would just as soon cut you as look at you.")

In truth, my unwillingness to let this guy come in out of the cold had less to do with what I thought of him than with what I presumed he would have thought of me if the roles had been reversed. I knew in my gut that if he had been at the machine and I had rattled the door, he would have leapt out of his skin. He would not have opened the door for me under those circumstances, and I would be damned if I would pay him a courtesy he would never return. "Just look at him," I thought. "He probably feels entitled to the air I breathe. How dare he?"

I turned around and continued with my transaction. To

my surprise, Mr. Cashseeker (for want of a better name) began
banging on the door. My indignation turned to wrath. I spun
around, flipped him the bird, and stared at him venomously.
Startled, he stepped away from the door. Satisfied that he had
gotten the message, I completed the withdrawal. I did not,
however, feel triumphant. In fact, I felt totally unnerved. My
heart started to pound, my hands began to shake. I got control
of myself, tucked my card in my wallet and my money in my
pocket, and turned around once again.

I held the door open, and a little too grandly gestured
for my tormentor to come in. He passed by me warily, looking bewildered and angry, and muttered something under his
breath. Although I didn't catch what he said, I felt compelled
to respond. I tried to remain calm, but the swirl of emotions
inside me virtually undid me. I could scarcely speak. "If it had
been me . . . you wouldn't have . . ." is all I can remember
saying.

Poor Mr. Cashseeker had no idea what I was babbling
about. As best he could tell, he had just encountered a crazy
man. I, meanwhile, had just wrestled racism to the ground.
But instead of bathing in the afterglow, I stood there feeling
rather foolish, for I was quite aware of how strange this all
must have seemed. There was no way he could know what I
was going through, or understand that I had just launched an
anticipatory first strike.

In addition to feeling insulted, I was deeply envious of
Cashseeker's ability to wander through life without instantly
being labeled "dangerous." I resented what I took to be his
easy assumption that he was perfectly welcome wherever he
went, and that he had a right to be there once he arrived. I felt

disrespected, as if he felt that I could not possibly possess anything he might want, and therefore had no reason to fear that he would take it away from me. I felt usurped, as if even the space around my body was not mine to control. I resented Cashseeker's obliviousness to the entire situation. I have to lead my life with my antennae constantly at the ready; meanwhile, this bozo gets to wander around in a state of virtual unconsciousness!

I have no idea what was really on Cashseeker's mind or in his heart. Perhaps instead of reflecting unconscious racial privilege, his thoughtless encroachment stemmed from the fact that he was a total space cadet (though that account doesn't explain the resentment he displayed when I initially signaled for him not to come in). Perhaps if the roles had been reversed he really wouldn't have freaked at the sight of a Black man watching him withdraw money from a cash machine on a dark and deserted street corner. But this much I *do* know. There is no way on God's good earth that I could have interacted with him solely as one individual to another, without at least subconsciously taking into account what I believe to be true about Black/White relations in America. And there was no way that he could have interacted with me in a way that was totally divorced from his own prior experiences and understandings concerning race.

Of course, there is another moral to the story. Often our assumptions hamstring us, and leave little room for people to act in ways counter to our experience. They so heavily filter what we see that it becomes virtually impossible for people to unfold and define themselves as they might wish. And on occasion, our expectations even create the very thing we least desire. As the protagonist in Genet's *The Thief's Journal* observed: "I felt within me the need to become what I had been accused of being . . . [I became] the coward, traitor, thief and fairy they saw in me."[2]

How can we avoid these traps? For starters, we should admit that our assumptions frame how we experience the world. Then, instead of pretending that we can engage others without prejudgment, we should focus our energies on putting our "priors" on the table. But first we must unearth them. This is often quite difficult to do, since we are frequently not even aware of them. In order to become conscious of our underlying assumptions, we should ask ourselves a series of questions: "What do I really know about this person?" "What do I think I know?" "On what do I base my hunches?" "How is she likely to respond to me and to what I have to say?" "What makes me think that?"

Owning up to our initial assumptions is often hard to do. I sing in a racially integrated gospel choir, the Salt and Pepper Gospel Singers. During a recent rehearsal, I noticed a well-dressed man sitting at the back of the church. We frequently have visitors—friends of choir members, people who want us to sing at some event or other, folk who are thinking about joining us—and I usually pay them little mind. But I noticed three things about this man besides his suit: he was sitting in the last row; he was very dark; and he seemed almost immobile. Soon, he became the farthest thing from my mind, for partway through the rehearsal the Holy Spirit began to really move in and among us. We always minister to ourselves even as we minister to others, but sometimes the Spirit just takes over. We "had church" that night.

As we joined hands for our closing prayer, one of the Salts in the choir announced that she wanted to introduce a new friend. She then gestured toward the man at the back, noted that he was a minister doing research in preparation for the founding of a new seminary, and invited him to say a few words. Slowly, he moved toward us, looking assured and perplexed at the same time. He started by explaining how he came to be there that evening. Sheila had described the choir to him, and had repeatedly invited him to take in a rehearsal. Although he didn't come right out and say it, he hadn't been able to think of a polite way to decline, and therefore eventually made the trek. Next he described his professional background, and outlined his vision of an ecumenical seminary that would teach students about various religious and cultural traditions, including African-American.

He then began to ramble, jumping from one loosely related topic to another. It quickly became apparent that something was weighing on him and he was trying to screw up his courage to express it. As he continued beating around a very large bush with no end in sight, one member of the choir stage-whispered, "Go on and say it." Several of us sneaked a peak at one another, confirming at a glance that we pretty much knew what "it" was. Finally, it tumbled out; our visitor had been reluctant to come because he assumed that White folk could not sing traditional Black gospel music. And he had been shocked to discover otherwise. He looked chagrined, and his face betrayed concern that the White members of the choir might be offended. He needn't have worried. They had been there before. They, and the Peppers too, were just happy that he was out of his misery.

Even when we manage to surface our underlying assumptions and animating concerns, we can quickly become *dis*engaged if we fail to treat each other's views with respect. When it comes to race, too often the opinions and judgments of people of color are regarded by Whites as subjective and self-interested, and therefore of dubious value. We need look no further than the legal academy to see this dynamic in action. At many schools, people of color new to teaching are advised by concerned White colleagues to avoid dealing with questions of race in their scholarship. "I just worry that your work won't be taken seriously," they are told. "First get tenure. Then you can write about whatever you want." Meanwhile, White junior faculty are given free rein to write about race. If they produce quality work that is supportive of the aspirations of people of color, they are applauded. After all, they didn't *have to* come out that way. They also are applauded if their scholarship is highly critical of positions associated with prominent scholars of color, and are cited for their "bravery." The assumption underlying all of this is that people of color have a stake in how the story of race is told, and perhaps even an ax to grind, whereas White scholars are merely disinterested, impartial observers.

This assumption was made explicit in a lawsuit against Sullivan & Cromwell, alleging that that law firm had discriminated against one of its attorneys on the basis of her sex. The case was randomly assigned to Judge Constance Baker Motley of the U.S. District Court, an experienced and able jurist. Before trial, the lawyer representing the firm asked the judge to disqualify herself from hearing the case, on the ground that as a female she might not be able to deal with the sex discrimination claim in a fair and impartial manner. Noting that

Judge Motley is also Black, the lawyer included her race as an additional ground for disqualification, on the theory that it might have produced in her a heightened sensitivity to discrimination.

In a judicial opinion notable for its restraint, Judge Motley denied the request, observing that "if [the] background or sex or race of each judge were, by definition, sufficient grounds for removal, no judge on this court could hear this case, or many others, by virtue of the fact that all of them were attorneys, of a sex, often with distinguished law firm or public service backgrounds."[3] It apparently never occurred to the law firm's lawyer that his White male clients were "of a sex" and "of a race" and that under his theory a judge who shared their characteristics would pose an unacceptable risk of bias against the female plaintiff.

Race and gender politics to the side, it is common for individuals to distinguish sharply between their own relative objectivity and the compromised perspective of those with whom they disagree. Most of us have little difficulty recognizing that other folk's opinions and judgments are colored by their position or their particular circumstances. For example, we take for granted that people who grew up in the lap of luxury are unlikely to appreciate the value of money. Sometimes, this ability to recognize other people's "situatedness" helps us to deal gracefully with those who have the temerity to disagree with us. We think to ourselves, "Of course she doesn't understand; she's never had to struggle." On the other hand, we rarely see ourselves as also being situated. We think that we pretty much see the world as it really is. Even in settings where we do not claim to be objective or impartial, we tend to rely on our own frame of reference as the standard against which all else is measured.

Consider, for example, Myra and Myrtle, mythical college roommates who nightly debate the merits of the male of the species. Myra's position can be summed up as follows: "All men are dogs. Some are into marking territory, others howling at the moon, but they are all dogs." Myrtle, on the other hand is of the view that "all men are pussycats. They think they are tigers, but a little pat here and a little scratch there and they all turn into little purr boxes." Though the debate is usually good-humored, it captures a quite real cognitive gulf. Myra is convinced that her judgment is correct, and attributes Myrtle's overly sunny view to her limited firsthand experience with men. Myrtle, on the other hand, views Myra as overly cynical, but is not surprised, given her wretched track record when it comes to romance.

My point is not, of course, to resolve the roommates' disagreement, but rather to illustrate how uncritical all of us tend to be regarding our own view of the world. It is the gold standard against which we measure other people's beliefs, judgments, and conclusions. We unconsciously treat our point of view as the norm, which makes contrary views "abnormal." Therefore, when we try to understand others without first understanding ourselves, when we strive to see through their eyes without first recognizing the limits of our own vision, we inevitably view their differences in a negative light. We criticize people for not being where we are "at" without considering the possibility that we might be at the wrong place.[4]

The trick, then, is for all of us to realize that we too have a point of view, a perspective, a set of experiences through which we view the world. We do not spy on life through an Olympian telescope, but instead are situated in the thick of things. Our judgments are as colored by experience as the judgments of those with whom we disagree. Perhaps men are neither dogs nor cats. Perhaps they are both. Perhaps they have no true "nature" whatsoever. Unless we recognize our own situatedness, we will never get at the truth, or come to realize that it has many faces. We will never appreciate the ways in which assumptions about objectivity and subjectivity serve to fix people in dominant and subordinate positions. And we will never understand why those whom we have put down might conclude that engaging with us is just not worth it.

Sustained engagement around race is also threatened by the profoundly American impulse to treat one another as if we were individuals first, last, and only. Personally, I don't want to be treated as a raceless individual. So much of who and what and how I am is the result of growing up Black and male in America. You can't begin to know me without taking my race into account. That doesn't mean that I am thoroughly defined by my race or that I don't value my own individuality. It's just that I didn't invent myself. No matter how unique I am, I am still, in part, the product of the social forces that surround me. If I had been born rich, or tall, or White, or female, I would be a very different person today, inside as well as out, at the deepest recesses of my being. In what way I cannot begin to say, because we human beings respond to social cues in an infinite variety of ways. In that narrow sense, we are all truly individuals. But respond we must, lest we become desperately insular if not autistic.

Nevertheless, people often try to engage with others around race while at the same time endeavoring not to take their race into account. The motivations underlying this effort are quite worthy. One is the wish not to presume too much about other people. A second is the desire not to put people on the spot so that they feel obliged to embody and defend their race. A related impetus is the desire not to strip people of their complexity by reducing them to their race. These goals are all quite worthy, even if the means chosen for realizing them—acting as if people are raceless—flies in the face of social reality. But there is a way to respect individuality even as one addresses group-level concerns. Simply put everything on the table. Own up to the tension. Acknowledge the risks. In a classroom setting, for example, one might say, "I realize that all of us have complex identities, and that race is only one aspect of them, but for now let's focus on that particular piece of who we are." Or: "I don't mean to put anyone on the spot, and anyone who wishes can elect to be an active listener, but . . ." Or: "Obviously there is more to who I am than being Latino, but . . ."

On occasion, people move from trying to ignore race to explicitly pronouncing it irrelevant. A typical claim is: "I don't think of you as Black" (or White, or Asian-American, or whatever). When I am on the receiving end of such a "compliment," I am tempted to respond, "Really? What *do* you think of me as?" Instead, I usually just head for the nearest conversational exit. If the speaker is someone I like, I prefer to remain silent so as not to embarrass her. If the speaker is someone to whom I feel indifferent or worse, silence seems preferable to sarcasm that can easily slip its bridle.

Ideally, we can all learn to avoid making comments that seem to e-race others and strip away part of their identity. But when someone inevitably screws up, rather than beat a hasty retreat we should seize the opportunity to deepen the dialogue. The question that usually forms in my head, minus the sarcasm, is actually a good starting point. "What *do* you think of me as?" Suppose, for example, that the answer is something like: "To be honest, I guess I think of you as White." The way would then be clear to explore what "White" means, and whether the characteristics associated with it are the property of one race only. If, instead, the answer was: "You are not like the other Black people I know," one response might be to try to convey the great breadth of the Black community. "There are lots of people like me in this very town." Or: "If you think I'm stiff and formal, you should see my Uncle Elmo." But there is also a richer, more subtle conversation to be had. If the statement "I don't think of you as Black" is perceived to be a compliment, small wonder that folk might think it wise to hide their blackness. Once the underlying assumptions are laid on the table, communication on a whole new level is possible.

Consider a third answer: "I don't think of you as either Black or White." That could lead to a wonderful discussion of what it means to have a race, and what it means to be oblivious to race. Then there is a fourth possibility, that the off-putting statement is simply meant to convey the speaker's pleasure at being able to really connect. "I don't think of you as Black because we seem to get along so well and I usually feel awkward around Black people." What a wealth of possibilities. "I feel the same way. Why do you suppose we mesh so well?" Or: "What is it that you usually feel awkward about?" Or: "Maybe you feel comfortable around me because I always sugarcoat everything I say." My point is not to anticipate every conversational gambit, but simply to suggest that awkward moments can become important turning points.

The very same concerns that inhibit us from taking the initiative can also distort what we hear. Too often, we listen defensively, just waiting for something to be said that is insulting or that places blame on us. Sometimes the anticipation of that moment makes it hard for us to take in anything else. Remember the scene in *Annie Hall* in which Alvy Singer, played by Woody Allen, and his best friend, played by Tony Roberts, are walking down a Manhattan street catching up on the latest. Alvy says, "I distinctly heard it. He muttered under his breath—Jew!" "You're crazy," says his friend. "No, I'm not. We were walking off the tennis court and, you know, he was there and me and his wife and he looked at her and then they both looked at me and under his breath he said—Jew!" "Alvy, you're a total paranoid." "What? How am I paranoid? I pick up on those kinds of things. I was having lunch with some guys from NBC, so I said to them, 'Did you eat yet, or what?' and Tom Christie says, 'No, Jew.' Not did you eat. Jew. Jew eat. Get it, Jew."[5]

I admit that Woody/Alvy is a little neurotic. O.K., make that a lot neurotic. But the difference between him and the rest of us is one of degree rather than kind. We all, at one time or another, listen as much with our fears as our ears. Some of us can never hear the good things that are said about us, but take to heart all that is remotely bad. Others filter out the bad and cling desperately to the good. When it comes to race, we tune into the slights, the put-downs, the aspersions, and the blame, and tune out the sincerity, the vulnerability, and the willingness to deal. We often recognize when others distort what they hear—"He sees racism behind every tree"; "She takes everything so personally"—but we have trouble seeing it in ourselves.

So what to do? Quite simply, the clearer we are about the things that sidetrack us, the easier it is to control for them. For example, I get my back up when someone accuses me of being insensitive or when I feel I am being unfairly blamed. I tune out of the rest of the conversation, listen for confirmation that I am being attacked, and more often than not launch a counteroffensive. On my better days (which is to say altogether too infrequently), when I feel my temperature rising I ask myself whether that old familiar dynamic is at work. If so, it is time to put everything out on the table. Once I describe what is going on inside me and own up to my, shall we say, heightened sensitivity, it becomes possible to discuss the thing that triggered my reaction without seeming to accuse my tormentor of high crimes and misdemeanors. Sometimes, my conversation partner cops to a felony anyway. Upon reflection, maybe she did unfairly blame me. At other times, I discover that I have totally misread the situation. But even in the great ambiguous middle, at least the conversation has moved forward and we have been honest with each other and lived to tell the tale.

It is much more difficult to proceed when the other person is the one who is filtering like crazy. It is one thing to acknowledge one's own testiness; it is quite another to call other people on theirs. Too often, phrases like "you seem a bit hypersensitive" are used to put others down and to trivialize their concerns. Of course, the greater the level of trust, the more risks we can take. The Tony Roberts character can say, "Alvy, you're paranoid" without undermining their relationship. Usually, however, we have to proceed with great caution. Also humility, since even paranoids are sometimes picked on. Often the safest approach is to acknowledge our own role in triggering the testy response. For example: "Something about the way that I am putting things seems to be pushing your buttons, and I really don't mean to."

Not only do we hobble conversation by excessively filtering what we hear. We also screw things up by filtering what others may say. Often we play a game of "I will only listen if you . . . ," which makes it difficult for others to speak honestly, forcefully, and in their own voice. We insist, for example, that they use certain words and avoid the use of others. "Don't use the term 'genocide,' it's too loaded." "It's not a 'riot,' it's a 'rebellion.' " "Use 'Asian Pacific Islander' instead of 'Asian-American.' " "I don't mind if you refer to 'some White men,' but how can you make categorical statements about all White men?" Terminology matters, of course, but too often we are less interested in coming to terms than we are in jockeying for position.[6] Sometimes, we lay down conversational ground rules that prize dispassion and gentility. For example, at a recent conference of law professors I ran into a woman I barely know who asked me what I was up to these days. When I mentioned that I was writing a book about racial healing, she demanded with startling vehemence, "Just make sure you tell people how to communicate in ways that aren't upsetting!"

Insistence on pain-free engagement can be profoundly silencing for people who have difficult messages to deliver. It also provides a handy escape route for those who don't really want to engage anyway. I am reminded of a particular four-year-old I know who regularly seeks to sidestep parental discipline by wailing plaintively, "Mommy, that hurts my feelings."

Sometimes, rather than demand that people not cause us pain, we insist that they not speak of the pain which we, or others, have caused them. We tell them, in essence, "I've got pain, you've got pain, all God's chillun got pain." The net effect is to level everyone's experiences and to insist that feelings, emotions, and consequences be parked at the door.

Finally, just as we can undermine meaningful conversation by failing to hear or by placing barriers in the way of heartfelt expression, we can also subvert it by failing to respond. When we do not match candor with candor or reward risk taking by jumping out there ourselves, our attempts to engage quickly turn to ashes.

It is not surprising that when opportunities for true engagement present themselves, we are as likely to run from them as to seize them. After all, we are taught from childhood to walk on eggshells when it comes to race. When I was perhaps twelve or thirteen, I attended Camp Insmont, a Presbyterian summer camp that drew kids from all over Colorado. I don't remember how many campers were in attendance, but I do know that there couldn't have been more than half a dozen or so Black kids, all of whom were from my church in Denver. Lots of the other kids were from out-of-the-way places like Strasburg and Gunnison.

I remember well one afternoon in which the campers and our counselors sat in a circle singing songs. In one of them, we made up the verses as we went along. Sung to the tune of "The More We Get Together," each verse began with "Did you ever see a . . . ? We filled in the blank by thinking up a noun (usually a compound one) which, when split apart, produced a humorous noun-verb combination. Needless to say, we did not understand what we were doing in grammatical terms; we just kinda got the hang of it. So, for example, one verse might go: "Did you ever see a bell hop, a bell hop, a bell hop? Did you ever see a bell hop? Well, here comes one now." The next verse might begin: "Did you ever see a cat walk?" And the next: "Did you ever see a play mate?"

After we had exhausted all the familiar possibilities, we fell silent for quite a while. Then, suddenly, an awkward little girl with wiry sand-colored hair and alert eyes started to smile impishly. In a confident voice that barely contained her pleasure, she began to sing: "Did you ever see a Negro, a knee grow, a knee grow? Did you ever see a knee grow? Well, here comes one now." I was impressed. The verse was incredibly clever and hysterically funny. But my delight was quickly overtaken by the panic that set in around the circle. To my great amazement, the camp counselors began to publicly chastise the little girl for being rude and insensitive. I can still see the look on the little girl's face—embarrassed, bewildered, crestfallen.

The counselors were, I suspect, trying to protect me and the other Black kids, but from what? We weren't offended; just jealous that we hadn't thought of it first. If they had paid attention to us, they would've seen that we were cracking up.

We knew, of course, that we were probably the inspiration for the girl's creation, but then we knew full well that we were the first Negroes (it was 1960 or 1961) many of these kids had ever seen up close. I have often wondered what ever happened to that little girl. I certainly hope that she did not internalize the lesson to bite her tongue. I wonder what verses she would make up today. I've got one for her. "Did you ever see a back lash?"

I wrote (E-mailed, actually) my sister to see if she remembered this incident and to find out the name of the tune the camp song was set to. Valerie supplied the title and then added that she thought the original lyrics were kind of interesting.

> The more we get together, together, together,
> The more we get together, the happier we'll be.
> 'Cause your friends are my friends and my friends are
> your friends,
> The more we get together, the happier we'll be.

The words are so simple, so innocent, so naive. But maybe we could use a bit of naiveté, or at least a little less cynicism. I honestly believe that the song is onto something profound; yes, *the more we get together, the happier we'll be.* Not because we will necessarily become (or even aspire to be) friends, but because we have lots of serious work to do that can only be done in collaboration with one another. If we are unhappy with the present state of race relations in America, then we ought to get together and do something about it. And it is high time we got started.

As I observed earlier, none of us approaches the problem of race from a position of complete detachment. Therefore, whenever someone holds forth on the subject, it is worth trying to figure out where he is coming from and what he seeks to accomplish. We need to be modest and tentative about the conclusions we draw, for a person's "priors" merely shape the prologue, never the entire play. But understanding something about a person's background may enable us to control for undisclosed bias, interpret the ambiguous, and make sense of the otherwise inexplicable.

All of this, of course, raises questions regarding what I owe you as I speak to you from the pages of this book. I clearly have a stake in the issues I write about and my share of biases, predilections, and blind spots. My life experiences— who I am and where I've been—influence what and how I see. My "social location" influences what I choose to talk about. As a result, I find myself in a very awkward position. For although I am philosophically committed to the notion that writers should reveal enough of themselves to enable their readers to, in effect, look over their shoulders, practicing what I preach doesn't come easily.

I am a fairly skilled dinner-party guest. I chat amiably with whoever is near at hand, avoid lines of conversation that leave people feeling excluded, and in general comport myself as if I were on the host's payroll. I come to the table when called, eat what is put before me, and almost always use the right fork if there is more than one.

But what I am really good at—a veritable master, in fact —is the self-guided house tour. I live for the moment the host says, "Feel free to have a look around." Instantly, I turn into a cross between Sam Spade and Columbo. With a studied casualness that belies the intensity of my interest, I check out the tape and CD collection, inventory the books, take note of the pictures on the bedroom dresser, and count the number of toothbrushes. Has the fireplace been used recently? Is the living room mostly for show? Are the children typical teenagers? Is the cat a member of the family? Quietly and efficiently I move from room to room, trying to discern as much as I can about the inhabitants' private lives.

I bring this same anthropological bent (less charitably called "nosiness") to my daily interactions with friends, co-workers, and even bare acquaintances. At the slightest invitation I have been known to ask the most intimate and probing of questions. Even in conversation, I like to look into people's closets, peer under their beds, and thumb through their photo albums. I am endlessly fascinated by the relationship between how people see themselves and how they want to be seen, between how they present themselves and who they really are.

One might imagine, then, that I would be fairly free with information about myself. Wrong! I have a well-developed sense of privacy and a long-standing aversion to "putting my business in the street." I come by these traits honestly. My late father was quite closemouthed, as a matter of both philosophy (a five-dollar word he would never use) and personality. My mother is equally reticent when it comes to personal matters, but her engaging manner and outgoing disposition make it easy to miss the extent to which she holds back. I take after Mom. Except that I somehow missed half the lesson. My parents were models of reciprocity; they respected others' privacy as much as their own.

My aversion to personal revelation takes many forms. At
work, I have occupied the same office for nearly a dozen years.
During all that time, I have managed to avoid decorating the
place (books and papers piled high on the floor don't count)
because I am afraid that people will then think that they
"know me" on the basis of what they see. I don't want to be
labeled, pegged, or pigeonholed. I don't want to be mis-
judged. In fact, I don't much want to be judged period. To be
honest, there are limits to how well I even want to know
myself. Self-knowledge and self-exploration have their place,
but mostly I just want me, myself, and I to get along.

O.K., maybe I exaggerate a little, but suffice it to say
that spilling my guts is not my thing. Which makes writing a
book of this sort quite difficult. How can I urge you to address
issues of race with openness and candor if at the same time I
am unwilling to let you peer into my own racial anxiety
closet? How can I ask you to take real risks that leave you
feeling exposed if I am unwilling to let down my own guard?

Well, the truth is that I initially tried to do just that.
Not consciously, of course, but my instinct for self-protection
runs deep. I was well into the writing of this book before it
finally sank in that I needed to put myself more on the line.
From the beginning I had included personal vignettes that
were revealing and evocative, but somehow I had managed to
skirt around anything that might leave me feeling foolish or
vulnerable. I had not wrestled with those aspects of my own
racial identity that are messy or unsettled, and I had not put
all of my fears and insecurities on the table. I had, in short,
created the false impression that when it comes to race, I've
got it all together.

Friends who read early drafts urged me to peel back more layers and reveal more of my inner self. One of them "called me" on my tendency to use humor or charm to shift the spotlight and deflect criticism. Another sent me a book review in which a well-known African-American writer is chided for having "sanitized" his life story and "[l]ike a novice striptease dancer (or an aging pro) . . . shyly refus[ing] to take it off, take it all off."[7] Still another friend listened patiently as I worried aloud that some readers would seize upon my shortcomings as a way of dismissing what I have to say. "That's a real risk," she acknowledged, "but isn't that just one more thing you should talk about in the book?"

The final blow was delivered by my life partner, Jill. She has been a constant and steady believer in this book project and has supplied energy and enthusiasm (not to mention ideas and perspective) when mine have flagged. On occasion, however, our minds have not exactly met. Each time the conversation was the same. Jill would ask with anticipation in her voice, "Am I going to be in the book?" I would offer a vague, noncommittal response; something like "I'm sure I'll tell an anecdote or two that involves you." Meanwhile I thought to myself, "I can't believe she is feeling so insecure about our relationship." Jill would then let the subject drop, and I would breathe a sigh of relief while silently vowing to someday pursue whatever lay behind the question.

Then one Sunday afternoon as we were drinking coffee and working our way through the New York *Times,* Jill casually mentioned that the "Hers" column in the Magazine section was especially interesting. I thanked her for the tip, and added "the Mag" (as it is affectionately known around our house) to my pile. By the time I got around to reading it, Jill had disappeared outside and was busy tending the garden. I opened the Magazine, deftly flipped to the column in question, and gazed at the drawing of O. J. Simpson that accompanied it. Then my eyes fell on the title of that week's essay: "The White Wife."

I read with interest Jacqueline Adams's account of the Black community's complex reaction to the prosecution of Simpson. She began by explaining that the Black community tended to strongly support Simpson out of fear that whether or not he was guilty of murder, he would be punished for stepping out of line in marrying a White woman. Adams then turned to her central theme: that Nicole Brown Simpson "embodies a little discussed wound in the heart of many African-Americans: the white wife." In Adams's view, "racism" has played a "twisted, pivotal role" in causing Black men to pursue White women. "Too many black men . . . are so insecure that they need . . . the ultimate trophy, the All-American beauty queen, blond and blue-eyed."[8]

I had barely laid the Magazine down when Jill wandered back into the house. "You're right," I said as she paused on her way through the living room. "The 'Hers' column is powerful stuff." Jill blinked for a moment, smiled, and then in a voice both light and firm said, "You've gotta deal with it." It? For a split second I thought she meant O.J. and Nicole. But then it dawned on me that she meant us.

I, of course, was well aware that interracial dating and marriage is an explosive concern for the Black community long before I picked up the *Times*. And at some level I realized that it is precisely the type of issue that a book like this should address. But until Jill forced the issue I was paralyzed by fear. I especially was worried that once I revealed that I had "strayed across the line," I would lose a large chunk of my Black audience. I have heard it all before. My marriage to a White woman, and a blonde at that, proves that I hate my own race; that I am disdainful of Black women; that I have bought into White standards of beauty; that I am insecure about my manhood. Less demeaning, or at least differently so, is the view that I must have married Jill in order to get back at White people by taking what they prize most. None of these judgments leaves much room for the possibility that I married for love.

I have no interest in trying to justify my marriage or prove my Blackness. Having lived through the "Blacker Than Thou" politics of the late 1960s, I know that that is an un-winnable (not to mention self-defeating) game. Besides, if I let myself get drawn in, I just might reach back and "show my color," as we say. At the same time, I recognize that there are deep and important issues underlying the Black community's widespread dismay over interracial marriage. How should the community define itself? What obligations do its individual members have to it and to each other? And to what extent is the very survival of the community at stake? I return to these questions at length in Part IV.

Once I let it out of the closet, I came to realize that my marriage has provided a testing ground for much of what I discuss in this book. Jill and I have had to figure out how to engage each other around issues of race. We have had to deal with the heavy hand of the past and the wounds that we both carry as a result of this nation's sorry racial history. We have

had to struggle with the reality of racial privilege in our relationship (just as we have had to struggle with male privilege),
and have occasionally been taken aback by how differently we
approach one or another situation, thanks to having grown up
on opposite sides of the color line.

I also now realize that my marriage may partially explain
why I am so drawn to the idea of racial healing. A generation
or two ago, Jill and I very probably would have lived in a
social world that was almost entirely Black. That is what the
vast majority of Black/White mixed couples did, given the
hostility that awaited them in most all-White settings and
the warm reception typically provided by the Black community. Black people tended to sympathize with the White
spouse, who often was cut off from family and friends. And
because eligible Black males didn't seem to be in such short
supply, Black women worried less about the loss of a potential
mate.

Jill and I probably would have managed well in that era.
I grew up surrounded by Black folk and, to this day, feel most
at home in their company despite three decades of living and
working in integrated settings. This was made dramatically
clear to me a few years ago when I visited New York's Greenhaven Prison as part of an ongoing law school project. As I sat
in the dayroom with thirty Black and Latino inmates discussing various aspects of social policy, it suddenly dawned on me
that I felt safer and more comfortable there than I do in the
faculty lounge at Yale. At least I was surrounded by family,
notwithstanding the great chasm in our life circumstances.

Despite her very different and very White upbringing,
Jill too would probably get along well in a mostly Black

world (though not necessarily at Greenhaven). She had Black friends before we met and has continued to develop Black friendships independently of our relationship. She works in a predominantly Black and Latino environment and makes home visits (as a mental health nurse) in neighborhoods most White folk only see on TV. She has a deep respect for African-American culture, and is very much drawn to African-American literature, music, and art.

The truth is, however, that we do not live in an exclusively Black world. Nor do we live in an exclusively White one. We spend an awful lot of our time, individually and as a couple, straddling one or another boundary, or shifting boundaries by our mere presence. And that is probably how we prefer to live, being both/and rather than either/or.

By this point in my life, I am rather adept at all this racial high-stepping, but I am increasingly aware of the toll it takes, psychic as well as physical. I find myself constantly monitoring the environment. Am I really welcome here? How much of me? To what extent should I be on guard? Against what? What do people make of me? Does it matter whether they get it right? These are the kinds of questions we all ask whenever we are away from home. We ask them about our individual selves, but we also ask them about our racial selves when we feel racially out of place. And for those of us who are partnered to someone of another race, the questions, or at least the answers, become even more complicated.

RACE

Every once in a while I run into a well-meaning soul who says, with a touch of pride, "You know, I don't even notice people's race anymore." Instinctively, I freeze my face and try to keep my eyes from rolling. I usually fail. When I do manage to exercise facial and ocular control, the tightness in my jaw still gives me away. I might as well wear a headband that says "Gimme a Break!!!"

I don't doubt that some people can, on occasion, not notice race. But all the time? In America? Should such a person exist, she would be a good candidate for civil commitment, for to not notice race is to be badly out of touch with a significant part of social reality.

When initially encountering other people, we *Homo sapiens* usually take note of physical features that are especially salient. Features that lack personal or social significance can, of course, be safely ignored, and probably should be, lest we drown in a sea of useless information. But information that matters is worth paying attention to. For example, were I to bump into a right-handed accountant wearing a white shirt and tie, it would probably be a waste of mental energy for me to mentally record those particular facts. On the other hand, were I playing tennis at Wimbledon against the same man dressed in the same way, I would certainly take note of his odd apparel (given the setting) and would be well advised to figure out which side was his backhand.

I do not, as a rule, tend to notice eye color, except when it is especially intense or when it varies markedly from the norm, as when I encounter a green-eyed Black person or a lavender-eyed Elizabeth Taylor. Similarly, I pay scant attention to ear size and shape, Senator Paul Simon, Ross Perot, and Dennis Rodman notwithstanding. Usually, very little turns on whether I notice such features, since eye color and ear contours have little social significance in my daily comings and goings and do not play much of a role in my aesthetic judgments. I routinely pay attention to other physical features, including general body size and type. This may reflect a primitive need to assess whether the object of my gaze is a potential mate, an imposing rival, or tonight's main course (or vice versa). Less attractively, it may reflect my partial internalization of our society's fixation with the body beautiful—tall, thin, and taut.

I never fail to notice race or gender. That is because race *matters* in America,[1] and gender everywhere. Indeed, when the physical facts are ambiguous, as when we encounter someone who is racially unpeggable or a real gender bender, we feel compelled to figure out "what" the person is. I have learned, from friends who are the frequent objects of such curiosity, not to frame the question in quite that way. I even know better than to ask the question at all, unless I am invited to do so. But I have not developed the capacity to stop the "what" question from forming in my head. Recently, in fact, as I was chatting with a good friend, a David Bowie/k. d. lang look-alike walked by. As soon as s/he was out of earshot, Jackie and I turned to each other, broke into knowing laughter, and said in unison, "I know what you're thinking." Neither of us viewed the person judgmentally—androgyny is perfectly fine by us—but we were frustrated that we couldn't assign him or her to a category.

Such categories are as much social as physical. Although we usually focus, when thinking about race, on who begat whom and on the physical features produced by all that begetting, in truth race has much more to do with ideas and expectations than with chromosomes, skin tone, or bloodlines. Phenotype, the part of us that presents itself to the eye, is significant not for its own sake, but because it provides a basis for sorting people into meaningful *social* categories.

The physical attributes that we associate with race have no particular meaning in and of themselves. They are simply a means to an end, rather like counting off by threes or fours or fives to form teams in gym class. The process itself tells us very little about what game is to be played, what rules will apply, what is at stake, or what distinguishes winners from losers. We could play any number of games by choosing teams in this fashion. And we could choose up sides in any number of other ways.

When we play the Race Game, we choose up sides by color instead of counting by threes or fours or fives. The great advantage of such a system is that it minimizes cheating and can easily be monitored so long as interracial sex is discouraged. People cannot readily subvert the system by, for example, lying about what number they drew or trading numbers with unsuspecting dupes. In addition, sorting by race promotes intrafamily harmony in that it tends to place all blood relatives on the same social plane.

The object of the Race Game is to ascend to the top of the social pecking order. It is reminiscent of one of my favorite children's games, king of the hill, except that the Race Game is played in teams. Once a team makes it to the top, its energies are focused on staying there and on keeping others from reaching the same point. Teams at the bottom have but one goal—to climb higher. Those in between are constantly torn between maintaining their position vis-à-vis the teams below them and trying to climb higher. Part of the attraction of making it to the top is the sheer pleasure of being there. But in addition, the team on top gets to enjoy a disproportionate share of society's bounty.

For much of our history, brute force determined which team was king of the hill. These days, however, the game is played with much more finesse. Except in extraordinary circumstances, we no longer call out the cavalry (or even the National Guard) to settle disputes about who lives where, who goes to which school, who performs what kind of work, and whose labor merits what reward. Instead, we rely on an elaborate complex of rules, most of which are race-neutral, to establish the racial pecking order. Sometimes the rules take the form of laws, as when we create school districts or decide how public education is to be funded. Sometimes the rules are economic in nature, as when we decide what to regulate and what to leave to market forces. Sometimes the rules result from private policymaking, as when a corporation decides that its executives should have a certain look. And sometimes the rules seem to have no author, as when particular art forms are deemed "higher" than others.

Not surprisingly, one way to prevail in the Race Game is to control the rules. Each team seeks to define, interpret, manipulate, and, if necessary, alter the rules in order to improve upon or at least maintain its position. Usually, the existing rules benefit the team on top, which uses the power of its position to keep them intact. Sometimes, however, due to changed circumstances the existing rules cease to favor the status quo. When that happens, it is in the interest of the king of the hill to press for change.

Take, for example, the rules governing admission to elite private colleges. Early on, such schools happily admitted students with a broad range of aptitude so long as they came from the proper social stratum. People of color, along with the White Christian commoners and Jews of every station, were simply excluded. Over time, various social forces compelled elite colleges to become more egalitarian. As they became academically rather than socially exclusive, they began to rely heavily on standardized test scores even though (and in some cases precisely because) the tests tend to screen out a disproportionate number of African-Americans, Latinos, and Native Americans. Curiously, though, as the number of Asian-Americans with chart-topping scores and grade point averages soared over the last decade or two, many of the same schools suddenly discovered the wisdom of looking beyond the numbers and taking into account activities that reflect creativity, leadership, well-roundedness, or other traits that Asian-Americans were thought not to possess.

A second basic move in the Race Game involves the manipulation of attitudes. Just as slavery was rendered more acceptable by the false notion that the enslaved were somehow "happy" in their condition, inequality in contemporary society is made more palatable by self-serving assumptions and beliefs. Thus, it is possible to discount Asian-American academic success by concluding that "they are naturally good at math and science." Similarly, passing over Asian-Americans in favor of less qualified Whites seems less troublesome if we assume that "their immigrant mentality makes them overachievers." Both of these beliefs, while mutually contradictory, serve the same social function—to preserve the place of Whites atop the hill. Often the manipulation of attitudes is more subtle. For example, skillful wordsmiths have managed to make the struggle for racial equality seem less sympathetic by recasting it as an attempt by "interest groups" to achieve "special treatment."

The Race Game is a strange game indeed. It is often played reflexively, its players scarcely aware that they are engaged in active competition. In this respect, it resembles lots of other social games, including sibling rivalry and "let's impress the boss." Many players don't think of themselves as being part of a team or as gaining or losing based on how other team members do. They are rather like Olympic gymnasts who think only in terms of the individual competition and are oblivious to the fact that team scores are being kept as well. Finally, the Race Game seems to be never-ending. Unlike king of the hill, it does not end at nightfall or when our parents summon us home for dinner.

Given the objectives of the Race Game, to not notice

race is to miss one of the central ways in which power, position, and material well-being are distributed in our society. To
not notice race is to be oblivious to the concerns of those
below us in the pecking order and to lower our defenses
against those above. For people of color, to not notice race is
to fail to differentiate between those who are likely to come to
our rescue and those who are likely to abandon us when things
get thick.

On occasion, in settings that are truly egalitarian or in
which there is an overriding common denominator, all of us
can let go of race. For folks with adjoining plots in a community garden, race is decidedly less important than whether
your neighbor has any tips for dealing with aphids and Japanese beetles. In an airplane that is encountering heavy turbu-
lence, I feel a kinship with the other passengers that far transcends mere matters of pigmentation and social position. At
the annual picnic at the boss's estate, amidst shared feelings of
discomfort, awe, curiosity, and envy, one is more apt to notice
the "We're not in Kansas anymore" look on a co-worker's face
than the color of her skin.

But even in settings that bring out our sameness, we
often fear that at any moment the bubble will burst; that
something will happen to cause others to notice our race and
to treat it as significant. To stave off that day, we Black folk
expend enormous amounts of energy trying to make Whites
feel comfortable around us. We monitor our behavior so as to
avoid tapping into subliminal anxieties or fears and steer the
conversation to topics that are determinedly safe. We thus
achieve a measure of racial invisibility, but at a price—the
setting aside of much that is racially distinctive about us. Like
gay men and lesbians (of every color) who delete gender-

revealing pronouns when discussing romance in mixed company, people of color (of every sexual orientation) achieve color blindness only by closeting important aspects of ourselves.

Many Whites also fear the bursting bubble. They too long for the chance to escape assumptions and expectations rooted in race. They too would prefer not to be judged guilty by association—with slaveholders, White supremacists, and politicians who gleefully polarize the electorate along racial lines. During those magical moments when racial differences seem to melt away, they dread the prospect that their Whiteness will somehow become visible again.

Ironically, the more successful we are at being truly oblivious to race, the more likely we are to trip over it. For when we cease to be watchful, we occasionally say what we really think. Much of what is most heartfelt about race is rarely uttered in mixed company. We fear saying out loud the kinds of things that Jadwiga Sutak said to me. But we sometimes speak in categorical and unflattering terms when "they" (whoever they happen to be) are not around.

When we ignore the race of those we deal with, it is as if "they" are around and not around at the same time. On occasion, I have been in the company of White folk who momentarily forgot that I was present, or who were temporarily blind to "what" I am. It is as if I had been transformed into a fly on the wall. "If a White person had done that, he would have been out on his ear!" "They have no respect for family." "Did you hear the one about . . . ?" Suddenly, the conversation screeches to a halt and everyone freezes. Apparently, I have become visible again. Faces redden, and an effort is made to smooth things over.

The apology usually takes one of three forms. The most

straightforward version is: "I'm really sorry, I forgot you were here." More often I am told, "I didn't mean it the way it sounded." The third response is easily the most maddening: "I wasn't including you. I really don't think of you as Black." Apparently, Black people cannot be law professors or speakers of standard English or whatever else it is about me that prompts such a statement. The erasure of my Blackness is meant to be a compliment, but I am not flattered. For when I am e-raced, I am denied an identity that is meaningful to me and am separated from people who are my flesh and blood. If I embrace the "compliment" by letting it pass without comment, I am put in the curious position of disavowing and denigrating myself. On the other hand, if I challenge it, I am made to feel like a skunk at a garden party. At such moments, I am sorely tempted to show my admirers just how Black I can be.

I have also witnessed the reverse scenario, where Black folk have allowed a White friend to be the fly on the wall as they talk uninhibitedly about race. The conversation often includes unflattering characterizations of Whites as a whole. "It just goes to show you that Crackers will never cut you any slack," for example. Such comments are rarely inadvertent— part of surviving in a racially hostile world is learning to never let your guard down all the way. Everyone knows there is a White person within earshot, but the word has spread that she is "O.K." Consequently, the conversation usually continues on without apology. Only if the White person looks uncomfortable is an effort made to say something "reassuring," like "Oh, I don't think of you as White."

At such moments, I have noticed in the faces of White

friends what seems to be an odd mix of delight and discomfort. My guess is that they are flattered by their honorary non-White status. At the same time, I suspect that that status has a perverse countereffect: it causes them to reflect on the extent to which they really *are* White. And to the degree they wind up identifying with their race or at least concluding that their Black friends' indictment of it is too broad, they must feel strangely conflicted and more than a little confused.

We should relish these moments of extreme awkwardness and confusion, for they have the potential to teach us much about how race affects our lives. I speak with the zealousness of the convert. For most of my life, I have resolved the tension between wanting to say something, on the one hand, and not wanting to seriously embarrass folk, on the other, by biting my tongue. I am increasingly of the view, however, that once the fig leaf has fallen, we might as well look at what it has been hiding. For it is by exploring the things we dare not say to each other that we can best get to know one another. Just think how "real" the conversation could get if the next time someone says, "I don't think of you as Black," I respond, "That's because I only show you certain sides of myself. I don't feel safe enough around you to display more." Imagine the doors that might open if a person upon whom honorary non-White status has been granted were to say: "I know this sounds strange, but somehow I've never felt whiter in my whole life than at this moment."

Racial Identity

In the United States, who falls into which racial category is no simple matter. Once upon a time, there were strict laws governing such things. The laws were not uniform from state to state or from race to race. For example, a state might take one approach when differentiating between Blacks and Whites, and an entirely different approach when defining Native Americans. Nevertheless, the core idea was always the same; racial definitions were rooted in ancestry. The central question was whether one's ancestors hailed from Europe, Asia, Africa, or the Americas.

Complications arose with respect to mixed heritage. Though different answers were supplied at different times, in different contexts, and for different racial combinations, it quickly became settled law everywhere that Black plus White equals Black. In its extreme form, the rule of hypodescent decreed that even a single drop of Black blood makes a person Black. During slavery, the "one-drop rule" made considerable practical sense; the mixed-race offspring of predatory slavemasters became additions to the workforce rather than potential heirs. But practicalities to the side, the "one-drop rule" and the blood metaphor on which it rests transmit a powerful message: Black people are profoundly and unredeemably tainted.

With the decline of state-sanctioned segregation, the reasons for fixing racial categories and slotting people into them have shifted radically. Among them are that particular groups can be targeted in an effort to remedy the effects of past discrimination and that health promotion and disease prevention messages can be conveyed in ways that are culturally appropriate. At the federal level, the job of defining race is lodged in the executive branch's Office of Management and Budget. OMB's primary statement on the subject, OMB Directive 15,[2] spends most of its life in bureaucratic obscurity. But every ten years Directive 15 looms large, because it forms the basis for the racial categories used by the Census Bureau.

Directive 15 sets out five categories—American Indian/ Alaskan Native; Asian Pacific Islander; Black, non-Hispanic; Hispanic; and White, non-Hispanic. There is little uniformity in the way in which the membership of the categories is described. Asian Pacific Islanders, for example, are defined solely in terms of their region of origin. Whites are also defined by region of origin, but their definition also explicitly excludes Hispanics. Hispanics, in turn, are defined by a combination of region and culture. The result is a conceptual mess.[3] But the OMB gnomes were not striving for conceptual purity nor were they trying to describe biologically or anthropologically distinct peoples. They were simply attempting to capture existing social arrangements and understandings.

Take the "Hispanic" classification, for example. People who trace their heritage to Latin America constitute a classic ethnic group. Broadly speaking, they share a common language, common geographic origins, and a common culture. On the other hand, Hispanics differ from most other ethnic groups in that their racial heritage is quite mixed. Despite the echoes of Spain in the name, many Hispanics are not primarily European in origin. As a group, their ancestry is "tainted" by the fact that the conquistadores and Spanish settlers mixed freely with Native Americans and (to a lesser extent) displaced Africans. Rather than sort out who among this hodgepodge should be thought of as White, Black, or Red, most Americans tend to view the entire ethnic group as if it were a distinct race. On the street and in daily life, Hispanics (unlike, say, Italian-Americans) are treated as if they were part of the racial pecking order. It is therefore not surprising that OMB Directive 15, while specifically acknowledging that Hispanics comprise an ethnic rather than a racial group, places them on a par with four distinctly racial categories.

Given that race is a social rather than a physical fact of life, if the government is going to be in the race-defining business it makes little sense to proceed other than by reference to social practice. But that, of course, is a big "if," one which currently is being hotly debated in light of the approaching Census. For many people, myself included, the existing categories reflect an important aspect of our identity. To fiddle with them would be, in a sense, to fiddle with who we understand ourselves to be. At a minimum, it would deny our lived reality. For others, including a growing subset of mixed-race folk who prefer to identify with all aspects of their heritage, the existing categories do not reflect their felt identity. Adding a multiracial category or permitting people to check off more than one box would allow them to feel reflected in the national mirror that is the Census. Issues of identity to the side, the chief difference between those who would preserve formal racial categories and those who would eliminate them altogether is that the former are concerned primarily with ameliorating past racial wrongs (through, for example, minority business set-asides, targeted health promotion programs, and electoral reforms), whereas the latter worry most about not projecting present social arrangements into the future.

When it comes to determining what category a particular person falls into, we rely at various times on appearances, behavior (e.g., where a person lives, how she speaks, whom she hangs out with), and self-report. For example, when tracking race for statistical, epidemiological, or other similar purposes, the government utilizes the latter, although, as Susan Graham discovered to her dismay, in cases of noncooperation the relevant official is sometimes authorized to reach a conclusion based on appearances. "I could not make a race choice from the basic categories when I enrolled my son in kindergarten in Georgia. The only choice I had, like most other parents of multiracial children, was to leave race blank. I later found that my child's teacher was instructed to choose for him based on her knowledge and observation of [him]."[4]

In everyday life, we rely on appearances and behavior, especially when we are dealing with strangers. In cases of racial ambiguity, however, we tend to accept what people say they are. If they do not volunteer information about their ancestry, we are put in the awkward position of either asking outright, which suggests that the answer somehow matters to us, or leaving our curiosity unsatisfied. Most of us steer a middle course; we ask a series of indirect and roundabout questions designed to uncover clues.

We have little choice. Our government, fortunately, has never seen fit to establish racial identity cards, with the possible exception of birth certificates. In most parts of the country, we are much too mobile to know firsthand everyone's family tree. Nor is it as easy as it once was to infer a person's race from her social setting. As housing segregation breaks down (albeit slowly), we can no longer be certain that our neighbors are just like us. Our co-workers are even more likely to be varied, and from what I can tell all kinds of people shop at Wal-Mart and at Saks. Likewise, it is not always easy to infer race from lifestyle or conduct. I am no longer shocked to discover that the law student whose Valley Girl accent I hear echoing in the halls is Latina, Asian-American, or African-American. I am no longer surprised to find that the b-boy on the corner with the knit cap, baggy pants, and pimp walk is actually White. So guessing race is harder than it used to be. Most of the time we can tell by looking, but increasingly we have to take what people tell us at face value.

In sum, official designations of race piggyback on social conventions, and social conventions rely, in part, on individual internalization of racial identity. More fundamentally, internalizing a racial identity is, for all of us, a key element in the larger project of self-definition and of fitting ourselves into the world around us.

When I was a kid, the process of racial self-identification was not a terribly complex one for most Black folk. Clear lines of racial demarcation and a strong culture in which to roost left individuals with little choice in the matter but also little anxiety. Whether "high yellow" or coal black, nappy-headed or blessed with "good hair" (as we used to say with little consciousness of the implicit self-condemnation), we all knew that we were Black. Those who were "fair-skinned" enough to pass for White, and who elected to do so, still thought of themselves as Negroes in disguise.

Biracial children quickly figured out which way to identify. Although they might occasionally catch grief from the

Black community, they had little if any chance of acceptance by Whites. Often, biracial folk were among the most militant members of the Black community, perhaps to foreclose any concern that their mixed heritage made their race loyalty suspect. Their White parents operated within the same social parameters. Often, they had been shunned by their own families for marrying Black. In any event, they knew that in order to protect their children, they had to raise them as Black. If they had any desire for equal time when it came to their children's racial identity, they squelched it.

Then, as now, White people also tended to take their racial self-identity for granted. They were probably less conscious about it than Blacks, but their racial identity was rarely in doubt. Some of my White friends from school would have preferred not to be part of any race, and none of them wished to be associated with the likes of Bull Connor and Lester Maddox, but they had no confusion regarding which box to check despite the fact that many demographers opine that the vast majority of Americans officially designated as White have Black ancestors.[5] It never seriously occurred to my classmates, I suspect, or to most White people today for that matter, that thanks to the sexual meanderings of some distant relative they might be technically Black.

When that possibility is raised, the reaction is often far from indifferent. In an essay entitled "Passing for White, Passing for Black," Adrian Piper writes:

When I was an undergraduate . . . I worked with a fellow music student—white—in the music library. I remember his reaction when I relayed to him an article I'd recently read arguing that Beethoven had African ancestry.

Beethoven was one of his heroes, and his vehement derision
was completely out of proportion to the scholarly worth of
the hypothesis. But when I suggested that he wouldn't be
so skeptical if the claim were that Beethoven had some
Danish ancestry, he fell silent. . . . More recently, I pre-
miered at a gallery a video installation exploring the issue
of African ancestry among white Americans. A white male
viewer commenced to kick the furniture, mutter audibly
that he was white and was going to stay that way, and start
a fistfight with my dealer.[6]

In a thoughtful family memoir entitled *The Sweeter the Juice,*
Shirlee Taylor Haizlip recounts her efforts to fill in the missing branches of her family tree, and in particular to locate
relatives whose ascendants had elected to cross the color line
and "pass" for White. While their reactions to the news varied, many of Haizlip's ostensibly White relatives did not respond with equanimity.[7]

These days, racial self-definition is not a foregone conclusion for an increasingly large number of people of color. Biracial children, for example, are often eager to acknowledge
both sides of their heritage, thanks to a climate of tolerance
that did not exist thirty years ago. Especially for those reared
in a predominantly White setting, the notion that half their
background doesn't count seems strange indeed. Moreover, in
such settings the White parent often takes a very different
view of identity questions from what was the case in prior
generations. She is more likely to worry about being rejected
by her own child because of her race than she is about whether
the child will be accepted by society.

Similarly, children of color who are adopted by Whites as babies or in their tender years sometimes have difficulty settling into a racial identity. It is one thing to discover, intellectually, that you are African-American or Navajo or Thai. It is quite another to *feel* your racial and cultural identity. Again, the dilemma is most acute for children raised in an all-White (or nearly so) environment. Often there is a radical disjunction between the identity they know is theirs and the one they actually experience. If they are treated as if they are White in meaningful ways, what does it mean to say that they are not? This is a dilemma sometimes faced even by children who live with, and are of the same race as, their biological parents. Take Carlton and Hilary, for example, Will Smith's wannabe cousins on TV's *Fresh Prince of Bel-Air.* They are the products of well-meaning politically conscious parents who, in their zeal to shield their children from racism and provide them unlimited opportunity, have produced a pair of raceless ciphers. It is not just that they (especially Hilary) don't "act Black," whatever that might mean, but rather that they don't seem to experience themselves as being Black. And while it is sometimes useful to distinguish between fiction and reality, in my professional role I encounter kinder and gentler versions of Hilary and Carlton every day.

Young people are not the only ones struggling with issues of racial identity. So, too, are many people who thought they had settled the question years ago. Among the more thoughtful of them is my friend Trina, whom I have known for some thirty years. We first met at a fancy gathering in honor of selected high school seniors from around the country. Like me, Trina reflexively scanned the room looking for other

Black faces in hopes of finding safety in numbers. However, she had one advantage, for although it was easy for Trina to spot me and the other three or four Black folk, Trina was not so readily detectable. In fact, it was not until she announced her race that I had a clue. I might have guessed Latina, but more likely I would have said White. And given her ancestry —her father is a dark-skinned Cuban, her mother Italian— small wonder I was not certain.

As it turned out, we were headed for the same college, so we compared notes, promised to look each other up, and actually did. As our friendship developed, I discovered that Trina had a vast repertoire of ways of signaling that she is Black. In addition to making it easier to connect with the people with whom she felt the greatest kinship, these declarations doubtless saved many a White person from making an embarrassing gaffe. Trina was Black because her father identified as Black. Her race was fixed by his. On that point, Trina, like the society in which she lived, was quite clear. So strong was her personal conviction that even her daughter identifies as Black, notwithstanding her blond hair and blue eyes.

Trina and I lost touch with each other midway through college when she transferred to another school and moved clear across the country. However, twenty years later we bumped into one another at a conference and managed to reconnect. It soon became evident that in most ways Trina hadn't changed much. She was still one of the most straightforward, fair-minded, spiritually open people I knew. She was still inclined to try to hide her brilliance. And she was still exceedingly easy to be around, if a bit of a challenge on occasion. But something about Trina's way of relating to race was different. Although she continued to identify readily and easily as Black, she seemed much more interested in exploring the other sides of her heritage.

In the decade since, I have watched Trina continue on that journey. She has not forsaken her Black identity, but instead has added to it. And she has encouraged other multiracial people to develop a "both/and" rather than an "either/or" approach to their identity as well. Yet, unlike many who eagerly explore their multiple roots, Trina has not shrunk from her association with those of us who are Black first, last, and foremost. In the event of a racial war, I know where she will be.

Why is all this personal identity stuff significant? In part because it sheds light on some of the ongoing contemporary battles over whether and how people should be categorized. And in part because it suggests, if only indirectly, that racial boundaries in America are becoming ever more fluid. This is not necessarily a good thing, for such fluidity has the potential to divide communities of color along lines of complexion, class, and culture. There looms the distinct possibility that those who can operate comfortably in the mainstream will increasingly be granted the equivalent of honorary White status, on the condition that they disavow their colored heritage and embrace the dominant culture with a vengeance.

Once again, Hispanics provide an illuminating case in point with respect to both racial fluidity and its potential to cause worrisome fragmentation. Indeed the term "Hispanic" has been embraced by some light-skinned Latin Americans as a way of emphasizing their European origins and distinguishing themselves from others whose blood is tainted by that of

Native Americans and Africans.[8] Others have opted for the term "Latino" on the grounds that it is more racially inclusive. Labels to the side, there are doubtless many Hispanics who would eagerly embrace an offer of honorary Anglo status. If so, the impact on the life of the communities they leave behind would be tremendous. That said, the vast majority of Hispanics would, I suspect, continue to embrace a multiracial, distinctively Latino identity. Still others, many but not all of whom are dark-skinned, would identify as both Black and Latino.[9]

Just as fluid racial boundaries encourage psychological out-migration, communities of color exert a considerable inward pull on the wayward. That is because subordinated communities tend to invest considerable energy in policing their own. Such policing is designed to keep individual members from abandoning the group and to keep them from acting in ways inimical to the group's interests. The sanctions imposed for abandonment or betrayal range from public shaming to excommunication.

Every couple of years, it seems, *Ebony* magazine runs a story that is a variation on the theme: "Who's Black and Who's Not."[10] Typically, the story explores the racial and ethnic background of racially ambiguous public figures, mostly entertainers, who are rumored to be Black. Frequently, the subjects are quoted as saying that they don't like to be thought of in racial terms, or that they are truly an ethnic hodgepodge—Scotch-Irish, Jewish, Brazilian, and Trinidadian on the mother's side and . . . Those stars are, not surprisingly, treated disparagingly, especially if earlier in their career they seemed to encourage people to think of them as Black. If a picture of one of their dark-skinned relatives is available, it is usually given prominent play as a kind of silent rebuke. On the other hand, stars like Mariah Carey who own up to being part of the race are generally applauded, even if they insist on honoring other aspects of their heritage as well.[11] Almost as useful as acknowledging racial membership is acknowledging that Black people and African-American culture have greatly influenced one's life.[12] And if a star speaks of having suffered racial discrimination, she is sure to be embraced.

The letters to the editor commenting on these articles are particularly interesting, for they reveal much of what is at stake.[13] *Ebony*'s readers seem especially galled at the idea that people would pass for Black when doing so is beneficial (as when it gives them entrée to a particular audience or makes them seem especially hip) and then disavow being Black when race gets in the way. The belief that one should take the bitter with the sweet fairly leaps off the page. To do otherwise is to use the Black community by appropriating it to one's own personal ends. The criticisms are reminiscent of those leveled at Geraldo Rivera for adopting the persona of Jerry Rivers at opportune moments in his career (a claim he vehemently denies).[14] The readers also argue that the Black community is ripped off in a material sense when stars cease to identify once they have made it, in that they draw on the community's resources during their formative years but then give nothing back later. Moreover, they rob the community of its fair share of success stories and of the opportunity to bask in collective pride.

Finally, the unwillingness of some public figures to identify with "the race" is experienced by many Blacks as an

abandonment, an insult, a rejection, a putting down. We are
quite sensitive on this score, at least those of us who believe
that our community is exceedingly vulnerable, and are sometimes a little too quick to pounce on the prodigal son before
he even leaves home. If we see him rummaging around in the
closet where the suitcases are kept, we go on red alert.

This helps to explain a disturbing phenomenon very
much in the news of late: the fact that academically focused
students in many inner-city schools are taunted for "acting
White." Such taunts have the unintended effect of crushing
the spirit of some of our most talented youth, and spreading
the message that brains and Blackness are somehow antitheti-
cal. They are meant to convey the belief that bookish students
have wildly unrealistic expectations about the capacity of education to improve their life prospects. In effect, to say that
someone is acting White is to say that they are taking steps
that might work for White folk but not for Blacks. But the
taunt also carries a different and somewhat contrary message.
It is an inelegant and indirect way of saying, "I see you sharp-
ening the tools to make your escape from here. I see you
gathering provisions. I see you readying yourself to succeed in
the White man's world and to abandon the rest of us. I fear
that you are going to put all that talent at their disposal and
not at ours."

While putting people down for "acting White" is hardly
new, the practice seems to have taken on a particularly biting
and cynical tone of late. In my parents' day, Black folk felt a
sense of collective pride whenever one of us achieved success in
the White world. People who couldn't tell you the difference
between a contralto and a contrabassoon experienced sweet

pleasure just knowing that Marian Anderson had made it in the world of opera. Of course, artists who dazzled White audiences and thereby "uplifted the race" could not and did not (with a few notable exceptions) cross the color line to stay. They were, in effect, our ambassadors, and we welcomed them home with open arms. Of course, there were plenty of Black folk who thought they were better than everybody else, but "acting superior" was not necessarily equated with "acting White."

From grade school through high school, I was occasionally teased by Black friends for "talking White" though never for acting White. I remember the teasing as gentle in tone, though I am not above revising my personal history (unconsciously, of course) in order to smooth out bumps in the road. Back then, I was thoroughly bilingual—fluent in both Black and standard English—so on such occasions I just made a mental note to shift gears the next time I was around my accusers. I don't recall ever being "downed" for doing well academically. In fact, I had the good fortune of knowing that some of the hippest kids in school "had my back." I recall in particular a school assembly in which Rayford Tillis, an all-state athlete and the epitome of cool, portrayed me in a skit. He wandered aimlessly around the stage carrying a huge dictionary and memorizing fancy words like "endeavor." As we chatted afterward and remarked on his brilliant rendition, I realized that Rayford took nearly as much pleasure in my academic accomplishments and my admission to Harvard as I took in watching him go coast to coast on the basketball floor. If I had looked down my nose at other Black people or had run with a White crowd, I might well have encountered hostility. But achievement, and the desire to achieve, were not viewed as signs that one was preparing to abandon the community.

Today we still get a kick out of Black folk who can do battle on foreign soil, people like classical pianist André Watts, opera diva Jessye Norman, and even country singer Charley Pride. And then there is Cornel West, a scholar par excellence who speaks in a polysyllabic philosophical Euro-discourse that often leaves listeners gasping for air. After catching Professor West's high-wire act a Black friend of mine, who is no slouch of a scholar herself, commented, "I have no idea what the sonofabitch is saying, but I sure love to hear him say it." She then described West's presence in the academy as "like having a big brother around who can take on the bullies for you and beat them at their own game." She ended by exclaiming, "I'm sure glad he is one of ours."

Recently, the gospel choir in which I sing was invited to participate in a Martin Luther King Day celebration at the Apollo Theatre in Harlem. I was concerned about how a racially integrated choir would be received at that shrine to African-American culture until I noticed another group on the program, the Advanced String Ensemble of the Harlem School of the Arts. "At least we sing gospel music," I thought, "and once we get started we'll be able to reach the audience where it lives." But the poor String Ensemble. True, they were from Harlem and every one of them was Black, but how were they going to hold the audience's attention with violins and violas? I needn't have worried. The community's pride in the fact that these young musicians could hold their own in the world beyond Harlem's borders easily triumphed over any impulse to dismiss them for playing what might easily have been characterized as "White music."

The lesson of the Advanced String Ensemble's success is that what really matters is not whether a Black person talks, acts, or performs White, but whether it appears that she would prefer to *be* White. In other words, behind all the name calling and message sending are a set of fears that are captured by the following questions: "Does your way of talking mean that you look down on people who talk like me?" "Does your way of acting mean that you are disdainful of the way most Black folk act?" "Am I an embarrassment to you?" "If you leave here, will you ever look back?" "If you succeed in the wider world, will you share your success with those of us whom you leave behind?"

Unfortunately, such questions are more pertinent today than at any time in the past. Exit from the community is easier than ever. Life in the inner city is harder. Our culture is very much at risk because of the steady encroachment of mindless mass culture and because of the community's increased fragmentation. And we are constantly losing many of our most precious resources, as people who yesterday would have been teachers and preachers are today opting to be cogs in corporate machines that are indifferent at best to our needs. Given all this, it is not surprising that so many of us are so ready to assail one another based on the mere anticipation that yet another abandonment is in the offing.

Although intragroup discipline is perhaps most pronounced for Blacks, a measure of it exists within other communities of color as well. Just as the Oreo has come to signify folk who are Black on the outside and White on the inside,

Latinos speak of coconuts, Asian-Americans of bananas, and Native Americans of apples. By and large, Whites don't seem to worry over much about racial solidarity, probably because they operate from a position of strength. Save for the occasional crossover entertainer, why would anyone even want to forgo her White birthright? However, in situations where White dominance is challenged, steps are sometimes taken to exercise intragroup discipline. For example, during the civil rights movement of the 1950s and 1960s, the epithet "nigger lover" was regularly used as a way of trying to bring disloyal Whites into line. Friends tell me that more subtle versions of the same technique are sometimes practiced today when Whites are seen as being heavily invested in the needs and concerns of Black folk. "I'm just curious, what do you see in them?" Or: "What do you get out of being with them?" Despite (or perhaps in response to) this pressure, a fledgling movement has sprung up among progressive Whites who cheerfully label themselves "race traitors" and who actively align themselves with the interests of people of color.[15]

For most of us, the various building blocks of racial identity fit together easily. Our official racial designation, the label attached to us by society as a whole, our self-identity, and the messages we get from the group we "belong to" all stack neatly on top of one another. But for an ever increasing number of Americans, building an identity is much more complex. It is as if one block comes from a set of Lincoln Logs and the next from a set of Legos. The resulting identity confusion makes for a tangle of issues—social, political, and psychological—that is difficult to tease out, much less resolve. In addressing this new generation of race issues, it is imperative that we place on the table all that is at stake, and remain mindful of the ways in which our own "subject position" influences how we see and what we value.

Racism

A couple of years ago at the annual mini-conference for legal scholars engaged in "critical race theory," I was asked to critique a friend's work-in-progress. It proved to be a joy to read—chock-full of ideas and written with verve. But for some reason, I kept stumbling over a concept central to the paper's argument. Eventually, I put my confusion into words. "What," I asked, "do you mean by 'racism'?" The author looked at me as if I had lost my mind. The best he could manage was "Hunh?"

In retrospect, I can appreciate his confusion. It's not as if I hadn't used the same term thousands of times without so much as a second thought. But it was as if a once familiar shorthand had suddenly become strange. I repeated the question, adding that I didn't think "racism" had a single settled meaning. John blinked, then responded with more than a hint of exasperation: "Racism means [long pause] racism." Despite the fact that we were obviously shooting past one another, I continued to press the point until someone wiser cut in and redirected the conversation.

I have often thought back to that curious exchange. I was, I admit, a pest. In part my insistent questioning grew out of my role as an ostensibly naive reader. But mostly it reflected my own growing confusion regarding how best to understand the dynamics of race in America. Far from want-

ing John to clarify his thoughts, I wanted him to clarify *mine.*
For at some level I had become aware that my own working
definition of racism did not quite capture the ways in which
decent White folk contribute to the subordination of people
of color.

So, then, what *does* racism mean? One view—perhaps the
most common—centers on race-based animosity or disdain.
Racism equals disliking others (or regarding them as inferior)
because of their race. Despite its widespread use, this definition is deeply flawed in that it is indifferent to questions of
hierarchy and social structure. It applies with equal force to
the fox and the hound. Rodney King, if he hated White people, would be just as guilty of racism as the police officers who
beat him senseless. A Black loan applicant who has little use
for White people would be just as guilty of racism as a White
bank president who considers all Blacks to be unworthy credit
risks.

This evenhanded approach would be fine if psychic pain
were all that mattered, but race-based antipathy can have material consequences as well. And those consequences are not
distributed evenly in our racially stratified society. There is a
real difference between being insulted and being clubbed; between hurt feelings and radically diminished economic opportunity. Many thoughtful social critics argue for a definition of
racism that takes such differences into account. In their view,
the label "racism" is appropriate only when negative racial
sentiments are put into action and result in serious disadvantage.

Recently I have come to realize that there is a second
flaw in the traditional approach to racism, one that survives

even if we take consequences into account. And it is this: by treating antipathy as a necessary condition, we do not reach the behavior of people who have no malice in their hearts but nevertheless act in ways that create and reproduce racial hierarchy. That is why I embrace Professor David T. Wellman's notion that racism consists of "culturally acceptable beliefs that defend social advantages that are based on race."[16] Or, to rephrase it slightly, racism consists of culturally acceptable ideas, beliefs, and attitudes that serve to sustain the racial pecking order.

Of course, culturally *unacceptable* beliefs are also used to sustain the pecking order. At some level, White dominance continues to be justified by such crude claims as that Black people are intellectually inferior, Latinos are inherently lazy, and Asian-Americans are untrustworthy. But we rarely hear such "hard racism" these days in the boardrooms of major corporations, or in the well of Congress, or on radio and television, or from the pulpit or podium. Even conversations across the back fence increasingly reflect the broadly shared belief that bigotry is bad.

At the same time, none of us likes to give up the advantages we possess. We very much want to believe that we are entitled to them, or that we at least came by them legitimately. Sure, inequalities exist, but they can be explained. In justifying our superior position, we are constrained by the desire not to come across as bigots, to ourselves as well as to others. We want to retain the advantages we have and to feel good about ourselves in the process. And so we search for justifications that are "culturally acceptable."

A definition of racism that focuses on the search for acceptable ways of justifying racial hierarchy has many advantages. It gets us away from focusing on malice or ill will. It makes the racism charge less personally accusatory. There is a world of difference between being told that one's widely accepted assumptions and beliefs serve to prop up the racial status quo and being accused of harboring racial animus. At the same time, this approach eliminates a ready escape hatch; being pure of heart is neither here nor there. Finally, this approach mirrors how people of color actually experience racism. People wearing white sheets are not the only ones who hold us down.

So what are some examples of "soft racism?" The idea that affirmative action is bad because it stigmatizes those it seeks to benefit; the idea that a breakdown of values in the Black community is the primary cause of (as against being a reflection of) its misery; the assumption that one should monitor more closely the work of the new Latino employee because the strangeness of the environment might create special problems for him; the belief that Asian-Americans are inherently less creative than Whites. Ideas, assumptions, and beliefs such as these function to explain and justify why things are as they are, to absolve those on top from responsibility, and to feed dynamics that place people of color in no-win situations. To be sure, ideas that preserve racial advantage are not necessarily false, but given their impact they should be scrutinized with care and candor.

Defining racism in this way does not mean that we should no longer be concerned with prejudice and bigotry. But we have plenty of other words to describe that phenomenon. Similarly, we have words, "discrimination" comes readily to mind, for describing *actions* that place the members of one race in a less favorable position than the members of another. But racism can exist even where there is no discrimination and no prejudice. All it requires is the desire to preserve what one has and the capacity to form supporting attitudes and beliefs.

I would be remiss if I did not acknowledge a fourth, very different definition of racism. It emerged during the late 1970s and early 1980s, and was a direct response to calls for affirmative action to overcome the present effects of past racial discrimination. Suddenly, from the White House, in the editorial pages, over the airways, in the academy, and most tellingly from the Supreme Court came the insistent view that to even take race into account when formulating programs, policies, and laws smacks of racism. This is a thoroughly mischievous view. While some have naively embraced it as the logical consequence of a raceless ideal, others have consciously wielded it to destroy or at least undermine many of the civil rights advances of the 1950s, 1960s, and 1970s. In effect, this definition of racism treats as symmetrical the doing of evil and taking steps to rectify it. Thus, for example, racially restrictive covenants and affirmative action are treated as opposite sides of the same coin. Affirmative action may well be assailable on a number of grounds, but being the equivalent of segregation is not one of them.

HEALING

In a book of the same title, Wendell Berry refers to race as America's "hidden wound."[1] I like this metaphor because it suggests that the afflictions of the past, if left untreated, will sooner or later undo us. Sometimes dull, the race wound can be so achingly familiar that we mistake it for a natural part of us. At other times the pain can be so insistent that it takes our breath away. When things are quiescent, it is tempting to fantasize that the wound has somehow spontaneously healed itself. But then Los Angeles erupts. Or, less dramatically, something at work, at school, or next door blows up in our faces, and we are reminded once again that wounds fester and pain endures.

The central message of this book is that, if left untended, America's hidden wound will continue to cause us no end of sorrow. What is needed is a sustained commitment to a process of racial healing. To be sure, our public conversations about race frequently invoke the language of healing. Often healing talk is prompted by one or another ceremonial event, such as Martin Luther King's birthday or National Brotherwood Week. At such times, the term "healing" is a shorthand for coming together, setting aside our differences, and focusing instead on what we have in common. The language of healing is also regularly invoked in times of strife. "Now is the time for healing," intone our politicians every time something happens that threatens to tear us apart. Again, the underlying idea seems to be the importance of pulling together and putting the past behind us. Too often the language of healing is used to squelch frank talk about race. Such talk is divisive, we are told, and likely to produce ill will and discord. Instead of promoting divisiveness we should be promoting healing.

I am offering a rather different conception of healing. If engagement is the first step toward healing, then the second is pure, unadulterated struggle. Unlike those who counsel smoothing over our differences and pushing our fears to the side, I am convinced that the only way to truly heal the past and prepare for a more just future is to (as we used to say) let it all hang out. In this I draw guidance and inspiration from no less an American patriot than Frederick Douglass. "If there is no struggle, there is no progress. Those who profess to favor [racial justice], and yet deprecate agitation, . . . want crops without plowing up the ground, they want rain without thunder and lightning. They want the ocean without the awful roar of its many waters."[2]

I also draw inspiration from our brothers and sisters, of all races and ethnicities, in South Africa and the Middle East. Against much longer odds than we, historical enemies are engaged in the painful, halting, yet crucial process of transformative healing. I draw inspiration as well from survivors of the Holocaust who have revisited the concentration camps[3] or returned to their birthplaces[4] in order to come to grips with what happened there and, in the process, heal themselves.

Returning to Berry's metaphor, let us assume for the moment that America's race problem is analogous to a wound to the body. How should we set about healing it? The answer depends, in part, on where we think we are in the healing process. If we are near the end, as many race-weary leaders and just plain folk seem to think, then we have only to follow the advice we so rarely heed in our personal lives. "Don't pick the scab." "Don't worry the wound." "If you just leave it alone, it will heal itself." Come to think of it, that sounds very much like what we are told whenever a Jesse Jackson or a Ben Chavis or a Lani Guinier or a Bill Bradley seeks to bring the issue of race to center stage. But what if we aren't yet that far along?

When we sustain a physical wound, say a deep laceration, one of the first things we have to do is to clean it out and apply an antiseptic. (In the old days, we used to use iodine or Mercurochrome. If it hurt, you knew it must be working. I confess I don't really trust modern ointments because I can't feel them eating away at the germs. More fundamentally, there is something radically wrong with our modern expectation that healing can be painless.) After thoroughly cleaning the wound, we have to check the extent of the injury. Is there internal bleeding? Has anything vital been affected? Are there signs of infection?

After stitching the wound closed, we have to cover it with clean dressings that allow in air. But we can't stop there.

We have to change the dressings from time to time, check the stitches, perhaps reclean the wound, look for suspicious discharges, and make sure that an infection hasn't set in. If we don't do all this, we may never reach the stage of letting nature take its course.

Dealing with our racial wound is very much like that. Healing is a process that has many steps. Yet we try to move too quickly from the traumatic event to the day the bandages are removed. In our zeal to avoid inflaming the wound, we fail to clean it properly. We rush to close it, and do not check to see if our stitches have held. We ignore the possibility of infection, and convince ourselves that the occasional oozing is nothing to worry about. We cover it over with material that is contaminated, and leave the dressing unchanged for fear of what we may discover underneath. And so our racial wound festers. And eventually, like Langston Hughes's dream deferred, it explodes.[5]

It is helpful to conceive of our hidden wound in psychological terms as well. For in a very real sense, we are struggling to repair deeply troubled relationships that are the product of an even more troubled history. Whatever we make of the contemporary scene, we would all agree, I trust, that in its formative stages the relationship between America's White citizens and her various inhabitants of color was one of domination and subordination. The mechanisms varied—broken treaties, slave auctions, coolie labor laws—but the effect was the same, a hierarchical relationship backed up by state power.

It would be nice to think that at some point the depredations of the past will cease to haunt us, but abusive relationships have a way of reproducing themselves from generation to generation. Just as abused children tend to abuse their own children, we tend to replicate the racial roles we have experienced. Despite vast changes in our society, we often slide into familiar patterns. Those in control tend to remain in control. But their continued dominance comes at a price: a siege mentality and fear of revolt. Those at the bottom remain at the bottom, seething, and more than occasionally directing their anger inward. When we do manage to alter our behavior, our attitudes and expectations rarely catch up in time. Like someone who slims down after being obese all her life, we still see the old us in the mirror. We have difficulty believing that things have really changed, and run a serious risk of undermining ourselves.

How, then, can we break the grip of the past? How can we stop replaying old tapes and repeating old patterns? How do we unburden ourselves of the hurts, fears, anxieties, and woes that have been bequeathed to us? How do we heal our psychological wounds? By taking a leaf from Mandela and De Klerk, Begin and Sadat, Arafat and Rabin. Among the many lessons they have to teach us are the importance of candidly confronting the past, expressing genuine regret, carefully appraising the present in light of the past, agreeing to repair that which can be repaired, accepting joint responsibility for the future, and refusing to be derailed by setbacks and short-term failure.

Like the Holocaust survivors who returned to the places from which they had been cast out, we may have to travel back in time to painful places. We may have to confront things about ourselves that we would rather not admit. And eventually, we will have to let go of defenses that may have served us well for a very long time. The process of healing our hidden wound promises to be unsettling, uncertain, and arduous. But, then, struggle always comes at a price.

Once we have engaged one another and begun to confront our troubled past, we can turn to the final step in the healing process: planning the future. Again, the experiences of South Africa and the Middle East are instructive. Letting go of the past is never easy, but it is made appreciably easier if the parties agree to construct a radically different tomorrow. For if the future is inhospitable to the evils of the past, then at least they would not have been suffered in vain.

If we are to make good on the promise of racial healing, we have to build a future in which there are no permanent winners and permanent losers, in which race and social position have no correlation, and in which true equality is the norm rather than the exception. In short, we have to transform the very meaning of race. Finally, we have to figure out how to get from here to there, and to share the burden fairly, without sacrificing yet another generation of those who have suffered most.

PART THREE

What White Folk Must Do

WHITE SKIN PRIVILEGE

Most White people, in my experience, tend not to think of themselves in racial terms. They know that they are White, of course, but mostly that translates into being not Black, not Asian-American, and not Native American. Whiteness, in and of itself, has little meaning.[1]

For a significant chunk, the inability to "get" race, and to understand why it figures so prominently in the lives of most people of color, stems from a deep affliction—the curse of rugged individualism. All of us, to some degree, suffer from this peculiarly American delusion that we are individuals first and foremost, captains of our own ships, solely responsible for our own fates. When taken to extremes, this ideal is antagonistic to the very idea of community. Even families cease to be vibrant social organisms; instead they are viewed as mere incubators and support systems for the individuals who happen to be born into them.

For those who embrace the rugged individualist ideal with a vengeance and who have no countervailing experience of community, the idea that a person's sense of self could be tied to that of a group is well-nigh incomprehensible. Collective concerns can only be interpreted as "groupthink"; collective responsibility as some strange foreign ideology. I frankly despair of being able to reach such people. Fortunately, most Americans, whatever their professed ideals, know from personal experience what community feels like. They are meaningfully connected to something smaller than the nation and larger than themselves.

For some, the tie is to a particular region of the country. I have a former colleague, for example, whose West Texas accent seemed to get stronger the longer he remained away from home. For others, the connection is to a religious community, or to a profession, or to a community defined by shared ideals or aspirations, such as Alcoholics Anonymous and the Benevolent and Protective Order of Elks. Perhaps most significantly, many Americans eagerly lay claim to their ethnic heritage. It is, for them, a rich source of comfort, pride, and self-understanding. It provides shape and texture to their lives.

So-called White ethnics are not alone in this respect. Hyphenated Americans of all colors draw great strength from their ethnic roots, and take pride in those characteristics that make their ethnic group distinctive. Ethnicity is as significant a social force for Vietnamese-Americans living in Virginia and Chinese-Americans living in the borough of Queens as it is for Irish-Americans in South Boston and Polish-Americans in Chicago. Chicanos, Salvadorans, Puerto Ricans, and Cuban-Americans readily distinguish among one another even though their Anglo neighbors can't (or don't bother trying to) tell them apart. West Indians and U.S.-born African-Americans are as distinct from one another as steel drums are from saxophones. Lakota Sioux are not Navajo are not Pequot are not Crow.

On the other hand, from what I have observed, people who trace their ethnic roots to Europe tend to think quite differently about race than do people who hail from the rest of the world. Most non-White ethnics recognize that, at least in the American context, they have a race as well as an ethnicity. They understand full well that the quality of their lives is affected by these two social categories in distinct ways. White ethnics, on the other hand, are much less likely to think of themselves in racial terms. Like Whites who don't identify strongly with any ethnic group, they tend to take race for granted or to view it as somehow irrelevant.

At the same time, many White ethnics rely on their experience of ethnicity to draw conclusions about the operation of race in America. Drawing parallels makes sense to them because they regard White ethnicity and non-White race as being more or less equivalent. However, as the average Korean-American or Haitian immigrant can attest, despite their surface similarities, race and ethnicity are very different creatures.

Ethnicity is the bearer of culture. It describes that aspect of our heritage that provides us with a mother tongue and that shapes our values, our worldview, our family structure, our rituals, the foods we eat, our mating behavior, our music —in short, much of our daily lives. We embody our ethnicity without regard for the presence or absence of other ethnic groups. Of course, ethnic groups influence one another in myriad ways, and more than occasionally come into conflict. But they do not need each other to exist.

In contrast, races exist only in relation to one another. Whiteness is meaningless in the absence of Blackness; the same holds in reverse. Moreover, race itself would be meaningless if it were not a fault line along which power, prestige, and respect are distributed. Thus, during the war in Vietnam the North Vietnamese did not distinguish between Black Americans and White ones, since both seemed equally powerful with an M-16 in their hands. While ethnicity determines culture, race determines social position. Although the members of a given ethnic group may, for a time, find themselves on the bottom by virtue of their recent arrival, their lack of language or job skills, or even because of rank discrimination, that position usually is not long-term. *Race* and hierarchy, however, are indelibly wed.

Despite this distinction, much confusion is generated by the fact that for most American Blacks (excluding, for example, recent immigrants from the Caribbean), race and ethnicity are inextricably intertwined. The particulars of our African cultural heritage were largely, though not completely, destroyed by slavery. Part of what made the television miniseries *Roots* such a powerful experience for so many of us was that the protagonist was able to trace his heritage not only to a generic African continent but to a particular country, particular village, and particular tribe. We long for that kind of deep rootedness, but mostly we have to make do. From the remnants of our various African cultures, the rhythms of our daily existence, and the customs of our new home, especially the rural South and the urban inner city, we developed a uniquely

African-American culture, with its own music, speech patterns, religious practices, and all the rest.

The emergence in the 1980s of the term "African-American" was meant to supply a label for our ethnicity that is distinct from the one used for race. Most people, however, continue to use the term "Black" to refer to both. "White," on the other hand, refers only to race. It has no particular cultural content. In ethnic terms, a random White person wandering through New York's Metropolitan Museum of Art could as easily be Irish-American, an immigrant from Greece, a Lithuanian transplant, or a Texan on vacation.

Why do most White people not see themselves as having a race? In part, race obliviousness is the natural consequence of being in the driver's seat. We are all much more likely to disregard attributes that seldom produce a ripple than we are those that subject us to discomfort. For example, a Reform Jewish family living in, say, Nacogdoches, Texas, will be more acutely aware of its religious/ethnic heritage than will the Baptist family next door. On the other hand, if that same family moved to the Upper West Side of Manhattan, its Jewishness would probably be worn more comfortably. For most Whites, race—or more precisely, their own race—is simply part of the unseen, unproblematic background.

Whatever the reason, the inability or unwillingness of many White people to think of themselves in racial terms has decidedly negative consequences. For one thing, it produces huge blind spots. It leaves them baffled by the amount of energy many Blacks pour into questions of racial identity. It makes it difficult for them to understand why many (but by no means all) Blacks have a sense of group consciousness that

influences the choices they make as individuals. It blinds
Whites to the fact that their lives are shaped by race just as
much as are the lives of people of color. How they view life's
possibilities; whom they regard as heroes; the extent to which
they feel the country is theirs; the extent to which that belief
is echoed back to them; all this and more is in part a function
of their race.

This obliviousness also makes it difficult for many
Whites to comprehend why Blacks interact with them on the
basis of past dealings with other Whites, and why Blacks
sometimes expect them to make up for the sins of their fathers, and of their neighbors as well. Curiously enough, many
of the same folk wouldn't think twice about responding to
young Black males as a type rather than as individuals.

Far and away the most troublesome consequence of race
obliviousness is the failure of many to recognize the privileges
our society confers on them because they have white skin.[2]
White skin privilege is a birthright, a set of advantages one
receives simply by being born with features that society values
especially highly. Although I can't claim skin privilege, I have
a sense of what it must be like to possess it. I am, after all, the
beneficiary of male privilege. I didn't create it, I usually don't
seek it out, and I am often made uncomfortable by it. But I
possess it nonetheless. It is apparent in my dealings with auto
mechanics. It is apparent in the freedom I have to walk down
the street at night without fear of sexual assault, and without
being accused of putting myself in harm's way. It is apparent
in the respect that I can command in the classroom simply by
walking through the door. Not as much as my White male
colleagues, mind you, but a damn sight more than White
female professors, let alone women of color.

In a wonderfully insightful piece that has been passed along hand to hand by people committed to racial understanding, Peggy McIntosh describes how she came to realize, during the course of her reflections on male privilege, that "there was most likely a phenomenon of white privilege which was similarly denied and protected. As a white person, I realized I had been taught about racism as something which puts others at a disadvantage, but had been taught not to see one of its corollary aspects, white privilege, which puts me at an advantage."[3] McIntosh then sets out to identify "some of the daily effects of white privilege in my life." Among them:

If I should need to move, I can be pretty sure of renting or purchasing housing in an area which I can afford and in which I would want to live.

I can be pretty sure that my neighbors in such a location will be neutral or pleasant to me.

When I am told about our national heritage or about "civilization," I am shown that people of my color made it what it is.

Whether I use checks, credit cards, or cash, I can count on my skin color not to work against the appearance of financial reliability.

I can swear, or dress in secondhand clothes, or not answer letters, without having people attribute these choices to the bad morals, the poverty, or the illiteracy of race.

I can do well in a challenging situation without being called a credit to my race.

I am never asked to speak for all the people of my racial group.

If my day, week, or year is going badly, I need not
ask of each negative episode or situation whether it has
racial overtones.[4]

Not long ago, I gained insight from a surprising source
regarding what it is like to be confronted with the fact that
one is privileged. Sydney Patel is the American-born daughter
of East Indian immigrants. During her youth she never quite
fit in anywhere. There wasn't much of an Indian community
to plug into in her hometown; she was too brown-skinned to
be fully accepted as "one of us" by the White kids who populated her neighborhood; and no one else quite knew what to
make of her either. Mostly, folk just wondered "what" she
was. By the time I met Sydney she was a thriving first-year
law student. She excelled in the classroom, and outside it was
surrounded by a wonderful circle of friends. For the first time
in her life, she basked in the company of a lovely rainbow of
women of color. In many ways, they made her feel truly at
home, which gave her the courage to plan a visit to her ances-
tral home.

Sydney designed a research project, obtained funding for
it, and midway through law school boarded a plane for India.
Her goal was to study and be part of the fledgling women's
movement there. I will leave it to Sydney to describe, in a
forthcoming book, her extraordinary experiences in India, as
she struggled to come to grips with the practice of dowry
murder, and in particular the murder of a family member who
could have been her double. But what most interests me at
present is her relationship with the women she had come to
help.

Much to Sydney's surprise, India's women's rights activists did not welcome her with open arms. To them, she was first and foremost an overprivileged American. Although she had chosen to cast her lot with them, that was precisely the point. She could choose. She could choose whether to care about the plight of India's women. They had no such luxury. She could (and would) just walk away. This was their life. She could afford to join their struggle. They couldn't afford not to.

But there was an even deeper reason why her co-workers viewed Sydney with suspicion. Most of them were members of the so-called casteless segment of Indian society, a relatively recent redesignation for those who were once labeled "untouchables." Sydney, on the other hand, was born into a high-caste family. That social fact had zero significance to her growing up in Denver, Colorado, but suddenly it loomed large. To her co-workers, Sydney was the possessor of birthright privilege. Not skin privilege exactly, but caste privilege, which amounts to the same thing. Despite her good intentions, she was not like them, because they could never be like her.

"Now I know," Sydney said ruefully as she described the situation to me, "what it feels like to be a well-meaning White man." She was, of course, innocent in every sense of the word. Her intentions were pure. She had no desire to dominate her casteless co-workers. If anything, she wanted to learn from them. Nor did she have any control over the caste she was born into. On the other hand, Sydney exhibited many of the characteristics of privilege. She felt perfectly entitled to offer help to the Indian women's rights movement. She felt empowered to help. She simply assumed that she would be welcome. She had, as her co-workers so rudely pointed out, the freedom to decide whether to care, and the freedom to just walk away if things got sticky. And she always had the option, whether or not she chose to exercise it, of using her caste position to her advantage. Until Sydney faced up to the social inequality that was palpable to her co-workers, she and they could not arrive at a comfortable modus vivendi.

Sydney did not abandon the women's rights struggle. But she learned to accept the fact that there were limitations to the role she could play, and settings and circumstances in which her presence would prove more distracting than helpful. She adjusted to the reality of being distrusted on the basis of characteristics she was powerless to change, and used her newfound awareness to figure out ways to bridge the cultural gap. Finally, Sydney grew to appreciate the fact that she and her co-workers often did not see the world in the same way. Although disorienting at first, that realization caused her to become self-reflective in a whole new way.

It is often easier for White people to "get" the fact that disadvantage shapes the perspective of people of color than to get the ways in which *advantage* shapes their own take on the world.[5] Last summer, Jill invited her younger brother and his family to join us at our vacation spot in Rhode Island. At our suggestion, Dan and his son decided to try their hand at canoeing in the pond across the street. As I began to describe how to get to the "put in" point about a block away, Jill cut in to suggest that Dan and Lynn just portage the canoe across the neighbors' lawn. "Sure, we can ask them," I said with a notable lack of enthusiasm, "but what if they are not home?" "It doesn't matter. I'll leave a message on their answering which we can work to spread, and negative types of advantages which unless rejected will always reinforce our present hierarchies."[7]

That is indeed wise counsel. The key word is "hierarchy." Not only should we be suspicious of advantages that reproduce the racial pecking order. We should also treat as candidates for redistribution those advantages that are acquired in part because of a person's favored position in the pecking order. Of course, it is not always easy to tell when White skin privilege is at work. Nor is there an honest broker in the house. The wealthy want to believe that we can make everyone rich, whereas the poor want to redistribute income immediately. The one thing both groups have in equal measure is self-interest. Similarly, our initial judgments about when advantages can be "spread" and when they should be ceded may well break along race lines. That is fine, so long as we are honest about what is happening. Only then will we be in a position to search for a middle way. But no advance is possible until the existence of White skin privilege is acknowledged.

machine. I'm sure it's no big deal." I winced, but decided it wasn't worth causing a scene.

After the adventurers set off, Jill sought to assure me that she understood why I was troubled by the idea of traipsing across the neighbors' lawn without permission. She alluded to an earlier conversation in which I had explained my reluctance to go explore private beaches or peer into empty beach houses. I feared that, as a Black man, I fit the image of "perpetrator" more than that of curious beachcomber.

I appreciate the fact that Jill was sensitive to my frame of reference, but I am not confident that she fully understood that she had one too. Her view of the risks associated with trespassing was not just neutral. It reflected a certain sense of entitlement, a belief that she has the right to go wherever she wants, and a confidence that she is welcome there. In other words, Jill's assessment of the situation was every bit as much shaped by her Wasp upbringing as mine was by growing up Black and male.

It is one thing to recognize that one has White skin privilege. It is quite another to do something about it. That is the question Peggy McIntosh put to herself: "Having described it, what will I do to lessen or end it?"[6] I don't for a moment believe that the answers are simple. Part of the problem is that not all privileges are created equal. To quote McIntosh once again: "Some, like the expectation that neighbors will be decent to you, or that your race will not count against you in court, should be the norm in a just society. Others, like the privilege to ignore less powerful people, distort the humanity of the holders as well as the ignored groups. We might at least start by distinguishing between positive advantages

OWNING

"America has a race problem." Those five words seem innocuous enough, perhaps even a bit bland. But I can still recall how they surged through me the first time I encountered them. I was in my early teens, I think, and was hanging around the house waiting for dinner. While thumbing through the latest issue of *Ebony* magazine, I happened upon a serious-looking essay by historian Lerone Bennett, Jr. Instead of skipping over it in favor of something a bit lighter, I decided to check it out. I'm not sure I ever got to the essay's main point, for I was mesmerized by something Bennett said early on. He said, in essence, that we Negroes should stop thinking that *we* have a race problem and start recognizing that *America* has a race problem.

The effect on me was electric. Until that moment, I did not realize how thoroughly I had bought into the notion that racial injustice was "the Black man's burden." Sure, we could implore White America to set things straight, but weren't we the ones who were suffering? It was a short step from thinking

that we had a problem to believing that we *were* the problem,
and I was already in mid-stride. Lerone Bennett understood
how psychologically debilitating such beliefs can be, and he
reached across the printed page to save me.

Thinking of race as "the Black man's burden" is also
debilitating to Whites. It leaves them powerless to effect
change. It deprives them of the opportunity to be moral
agents and to participate in the cleansing of this nation's great
stain. It reinscribes a vertical relationship, even for people who
are philosophically committed to equality. Moreover, sitting
on the sidelines virtually guarantees that America's future will
be bleak. We don't have a person to waste. We cannot build a
healthy modern economy while disempowering and underval-
uing a large segment of the workforce. We owe our children
more; not just a thriving economy and a clean environment,
but also a nation free of permanent divisions and human de-
cay. As a practical matter, people of color cannot do it alone.
We are busy enough just getting by. Besides, the scale of the
problem is such that we need all hands on deck. In order to
redistribute advantage and rethink how we relate to one another, everyone's participation is needed.

So it is imperative that White folk accept joint ownership of America's race problem. But first they must *un*learn
the many ways in which they commonly *dis*own race. For
example, Whites often excuse themselves from taking an active role by engaging in a heightened rhetoric of Black responsibility. Sometimes it seems as if every race conversation
gets turned into a discussion of what Black people need to do
to get their own house in order. "They" need to become more
ambitious, to take education more seriously, to be willing to
meet Whites halfway, to stop victimizing each other.[1]

An especially galling version of table turning is "let's talk about Black-on-Black crime." I do not mean to suggest that Black-on-Black crime is not a serious issue. On the contrary. The Black community has viewed it as critical for years. Part of the reason that Louis Farrakhan is held in such high esteem in the Black community in spite of his many failings is that he has steadfastly taken the community to task for preying on its own. Similarly, Jesse Jackson has preached for years that there is nothing manly or honorable about victimizing one another. The same message has echoed from pulpits, podiums, and street corners in Black neighborhoods across America for at least a decade. Since 1993, Black-on-Black crime has topped *Ebony*'s annual readers' poll as "the most pressing issue facing Black America."

Given all that, there is something deeply insulting about the implication that Black people have not focused on the issue, or worse, that we aren't concerned about it, or worse still, that we wouldn't be concerned about it if White folk did not wave it in our faces. Moreover, there is something passing strange about the sudden interest in Black-on-Black crime to the seeming exclusion of Black-on-*White* crime. In any event, the dominance of this and other issues of Black responsibility serve to deflect attention away from our joint obligation to transform America's relation to race.

A second way in which White folk sometimes disown the race problem is by treating Black people as if they were fully in control of their own fate. "Why don't they just . . . ?" Why don't they just go get a job? Why don't they just move out of the inner city? Why don't they just stop having babies? Why don't they just exercise more control over their children? Why don't they just take the bull by the horns? (Does anyone ever say what you are supposed to do with the bull once you've grabbed hold of it?)

The problem is that such questions are often posed rhetorically. Moreover, even when serious answers are sought, some answers seem to fall outside the pale. Thus, it just wouldn't do to respond, "Because you wouldn't hire them," or "Because you wouldn't be interested in having them as next-door neighbors." Yet there is much truth in these answers. Black people do not, in and of themselves, control the real estate market, the job market, the economy, the welfare system, the school system, or the streets. The problem with the questions and the anticipated answers is that they assume a false world in which Black people are both the problem and the solution. The net effect is that the posing of such questions tends to deflect attention away from the possibility of joint ownership of both.

A third way in which White people sometimes avoid dealing with the impact of racism on Black America is by turning the tables. In particular, the notion that White men have suffered greatly at the hands of people of color (and White women) has been responsible for the death of many trees of late. "White, Male and Worried," proclaimed *Business Week*.[2] "White Male Fear" graced the pages of *The Economist*.[3] Perhaps less surprisingly, *Playboy* ran a two-part series entitled "The Myth of Male Power."[4] And *Newsweek* hit the nail on the head with "White Male Paranoia."[5] Actor/director Michael Douglas has even managed to create a virtual cottage industry with his portrayals of victimized White males.[6]

Assuming for the moment that *Business Week, Newsweek,* and the rest are onto something terribly important, we make a

mistake in allowing it to drown out or eclipse our concern for
the plight of people of color. Justice is not a limited resource.
We do not have to choose between doing right by one group
and doing right by another. Nor are the aspirations of White
men (or women) necessarily in conflict with those of people of
color. If we were to take joint responsibility for cleaning up
the racial mess, we could search for creative solutions that
expand opportunities for everyone. Moreover, upon reflection
thoughtful Whites might discover that sometimes less is
more. That has certainly been my experience as a male. Ceding the right to, as Humphrey Bogart put it in *Casablanca,*
"make the decisions for both of us" has been enormously liberating. Similarly, in a very real sense Black liberation holds
the promise of White liberation as well.

The attention given to the "victimization of the White
male" is troubling in a second respect. It is insensitive to
power and position and ignores issues of quality and scale.
Several years ago, lesbian and gay male students at a small
private law school in the Northeast which shall remain name-
less were the victims of a series of belligerent acts. Someone
had ascertained their sexual orientation (by, I suspect, taking
note of who received a rather distinctive party invitation) and
placed hateful messages in their student mail slots. Vulgar
graffiti directed at lesbians were scratched into an elevator
wall. Threatening messages were slipped under at least one
student's dorm-room door.

Eventually, the law school's dean called a town meeting
at which students, faculty, and staff could come together as a
community to share information and express solidarity with
those who had been attacked. As it happens, the president of

the university was in the building that afternoon, and was invited to join the rest of us in the courtyard. After listening to several gay students speak of how frightened, vulnerable, and angry they felt, he approached the microphone. "I know how you feel," he told the students, or words to that effect (I am paraphrasing from memory). "I know what it is like to be under attack." He then proceeded to describe the ongoing labor strife between the university administration and the clerical and technical workers' union and to emphasize how personally stung he had been when workers in the heat of passion had called him names.

The students stared at him dumbstruck. Although he claimed to be empathizing with them, it was obvious that the president had been unnerved by their emotionalism and was indirectly urging them to respond with more dispassion. But beyond that, how could he dare equate his experience with theirs? He was the president of an exceedingly wealthy university that historically had treated its clerical and technical workers as if they were vassals. He should be able to handle a little negative feedback. The gay students, on the other hand, were being stalked by an anonymous assailant simply for being who they were. They had no ready way to defend themselves, no sense of when the belligerence would end, and no idea how far things might go.

Equating the current plight of the angry White male with that of historically oppressed people of color is a little like that. Although the contrasts are not as sharp and the parallel is less than perfect, the error is the same. The comparison only makes sense if you sweep aside issues of hierarchy and control. Somehow, despite his vaunted victimization, the angry White male seems to have done rather well for himself in effecting a political sea change in 1994. Meanwhile, America's hidden wound continues to fester.

A fourth way in which the race problem is disowned is by simply removing race from the picture. "Wouldn't you agree," I am often asked, "that these days the problems of Black people have much more to do with class than race?" Before I can even object to the leading question, a follow-up is posed: "Wouldn't it make more sense to formulate social policies that target class concerns rather than racial ones?"

These statements (dressed up as questions) suffer from at least two fundamental defects. First, they assume that race and class are independent of one another and can be readily teased apart. Sociologists have long known, however, that race and class are sometimes interrelated in complex ways.[7] It's often difficult to determine whether what one is observing is a race effect, a class effect, a combination of the two, or an interaction between the two. (Not to mention the effect of mass culture. When it comes to watching the Super Bowl or purchasing Nike shoes, we are probably all more American than anything else.) Second, the sentiment that we should really be focusing on class either assumes that a forced choice is required or is a disguised way of saying that race is irrelevant. After all, if we aren't artificially limited to one choice, and if racism is indeed alive and well, then the simple answer is that we should focus on both.

As is too often the case, my fellow pointy-heads in the academy bear a measure of responsibility for stirring the pot. For some time, social scientists have been asking, in one form or another, the following question: to what extent can differences between the races (in attitudes, in behavior, in social location) be explained by class? The answer usually comes back that when you control for class, many or even most (depending on the study) racial disparities disappear. I do not quarrel with these results. I simply question what they mean.

Which disparities remain, and are they significant in the life of the Black community? Does statistically controlling for class tell us anything at all about what would happen in the real world if we sought to make the Black class structure mirror that which presently exists for Whites? How would we go about doing that? Would we, for example, employ economic (as distinct from racial) affirmative action? What would be the impact of this class shifting on Whites? If we could simply wave a magic wand and equalize the class structures, why not use it to eliminate racism as well? More fundamentally, why does the difference in class structure exist in the first place? Might not racism have something to do with it? And if so, what reason is there for believing that we can just focus on class without also focusing on race?

In fairness, I should note that some who suggest that we worry less about race and more about class are making a rather different point. They might well concede the case that is powerfully made in Ellis Cose's *The Rage of a Privileged Class*[8]— namely, that racism remains a problem for Blacks who break through the class barrier. They question, however, whether racism is an important concern of the so-called Black "underclass." Surely for the folk who can't afford to buy Cose's book, runs the argument, class is much more important than race. Therefore, by continuing to focus on race, we favor the relatively well-off Black middle class over the much more numerous and needy underclass.

Despite its surface appeal, this position is seriously flawed. Of course the problems of the underclass are largely economic. But that doesn't mean that the poor don't also suffer from racism. It may well take a different form than is true for the middle class. An underemployed single mother in the inner city is a hell of a lot less likely to be concerned about bumping against a glass ceiling than about being left behind. But the cause of her predicament is not solely her class position, for the racial pecking order is largely responsible for the fact that Blacks are massed at the bottom of the economic pile. And race-related indifference is largely responsible for our unwillingness to do what is necessary to improve the lot of the poor. Furthermore, while the material position of inner-city Blacks may not be appreciably different from that of, say, many rural Whites, the color line serves to divide economic like from like, thus increasing the likelihood that nothing will be done to improve their lives.

I honestly believe that many who push the "it's all class" line have the best of intentions. I also happen to believe that many others are simply looking for a way to get off the race hook. But either way, the practical effect is the same: to deflect attention from the enduring problem of race, with only the most theoretical of payoffs in return.

Finally, rather than disown the race problem altogether, many Whites simply make their participation in bringing about change conditional. I can't tell you how many times I have heard, "I'd be willing to help, if you would only . . ." Be less shrill. Get your own house in order first. Meet me halfway. (Guess who gets to determine where that point is.) Inevitably, I experience these preconditions as a kind of muscle flexing or throwing down of the gauntlet. In case I forgot, I am being shown who is still in charge.

That White folk would resist owning the race problem is

perfectly understandable. Dealing with race takes a considerable psychic toll, especially on those who are most attuned to
the felt grievances of people of color. To recognize other people's pain and to contemplate that one might have contributed to or benefited from it is not easy. It is no wonder that
genuinely decent White people sometimes try to make race
disappear. How do you make peace with the fact that people
like you have subordinated others in your name?

Then there is the small matter of coping with change.
For most of us change is anxiety-producing even when it
promises to serve us well. I suspect that most White folk
would be in favor of marked progress for people of color if
they could be guaranteed that their own lives would not be
significantly affected.[9] But that is not in the cards. We all
must change if we are to promote racial healing and aspire to
racial justice. All of our lives will be altered in some respects
—for example, our neighborhoods may change complexion
and our employment prospects may differ—but the biggest
changes will be in how we think. And abandoning old attitudes and familiar patterns of belief is never easy.

HORATIO ALGER

Ah, Horatio Alger, whose name more than any other is associated with the classic American hero. A writer of mediocre fiction, Alger had a formula for commercial success that was simple and straightforward: his lead characters, young boys born into poverty, invariably managed to transcend their station in life by dint of hard work, persistence, initiative, and daring.[1] Nice story line. There is just one problem—it is a myth. Not just in the sense that it is fictional, but more fundamentally because the lesson Alger conveys is a false one. To be sure, many myths are perfectly benign, and more than a few are salutary, but on balance Alger's myth is socially destructive.

The Horatio Alger myth conveys three basic messages: (1) each of us is judged solely on her or his own merits; (2) we each have a fair opportunity to develop those merits; and (3) ultimately, merit will out. Each of them is, to be charitable, problematic. The first message is a variant on the rugged individualism ethos that we encountered some pages ago. In this form, it suggests that success in life has nothing to do with pedigree, race, class background, gender, national origin, sexual orientation—in short, with anything beyond our individual control. Those variables may exist, but they play no appreciable role in how our actions are appraised.

This simply flies in the face of reality. There are doubtless circumstances—the hiring of a letter carrier in a large metropolitan post office, for example—where none of this may matter, but that is the exception rather than the rule. Black folk certainly know what it is like to be favored, disfavored, scrutinized, and ignored all on the basis of our race. Sometimes we are judged on a different scale altogether. Stephen Carter has written movingly about what he calls "the best black syndrome," the tendency of White folk to judge successful Black people only in relation to each other rather than against all comers. Thus, when Carter earned the second-highest score in his high school on the National Merit Scholarship qualifying test, he was readily recognized as "the best Black" around, but somehow not seen as one of the best students, period.[2]

Although I would like to think that things are much different now, I know better. Not long ago a student sought my advice regarding how to deal with the fact that a liberal colleague of mine (and of Stephen Carter's) had written a judicial clerkship recommendation for her in which he described her as the best Black student to have ever taken his class. Apparently the letter caused a mild stir among current law clerks in several courthouses, one of whom saw fit to inform the student. "What was the professor [whom she declined to name] thinking of?" she wondered aloud. "What does his comment mean? What is a judge supposed to make of it? 'If for some reason you think you have to hire one of them, then she's the way to go'? I could understand if he said I was one of the top ten students or even the top thousand, but what does the 'best Black' mean?"

Black folk also know what it is like to be underestimated because of the color of their skin. For example, those of us who communicate in standard English are often praised unduly for how well we speak. This is, I might add, an experience all too familiar to Asian-Americans, including those born and bred in the U.S.A. And we know what it is like to be feared, pitied, admired, and scorned on account of our race, before we even have a chance to say boo! We, in turn, view White people through the prism of our own race-based expectations. I honestly am surprised every time I see a White man who can play basketball above the rim, just as Puerto Ricans and Cubans tend to be surprised to discover "Americans" who salsa truly well. All of which is to say that the notion that every individual is judged solely on personal merit, without regard for sociological wrapping, is mythical at best.

The second message conveyed by Horatio Alger is that we all have a shot at reaching our true potential. To be fair, neither Alger nor the myth he underwrote suggests that we start out equal. Nor does the myth necessarily require that we be given an equal opportunity to succeed. Rather, Alger's point is that each of us has the power to create our own opportunities. That turns out to be a difficult proposition to completely disprove, for no matter what evidence is offered up to show that a particular group of people have not fared well, it can always be argued that they did not try hard enough, or

that they spent too much time wallowing in their predicament and not enough figuring out how to rise above it. Besides, there are always up-by-the-bootstraps examples to point
to, like Colin Powell, whose name has so frequently been
linked with that of Horatio Alger's that he must think they
are related.[3] Nevertheless, it is by now generally agreed that
there is a large category of Americans—some have called it
the underclass—for whom upward mobility is practically impossible without massive changes in the structure of the economy and in the allocation of public resources.

As for the notion that merit will out, it assumes not only
a commitment to merit-based decision making but also the
existence of standards for measuring merit that do not unfairly
favor one individual over another. Such standards, of course,
must come from somewhere. They must be decided upon by
somebody. And that somebody is rarely without a point of
view. Ask a devotee of West Coast basketball what skills you
should look for in recruiting talent and near the top of his list
will be the ability to "get out on the break," to "be creative in
the open court," and "to finish the play." On the other hand,
ask someone who prefers East Coast basketball and her list
will rank highly the ability "to d-up [play defense]," "to
board [rebound]," and "to maintain focus and intensity."

Or, to take another example, what makes a great Supreme Court justice? Brains to spare? Common sense? Proper
judicial temperament? Political savvy? Extensive lawyering
experience? A well-developed ability to abstract? Vision?
Well-honed rhetorical skills? A reverence for our rich legal
heritage? The capacity to adapt to changing times? Even if
one is tempted to say "all of the above," how should these (or

any other set of characteristics) be ranked? Measured? Evaluated?

The answers depend in part on whom you ask. Practicing lawyers, for example, are probably likely to rank extensive lawyering experience more highly than, say, brains. They are also likely to pay close attention to judicial temperament, which for them means whether the prospective justice would be inclined to treat them with respect during a court appearance. Sitting judges are also likely to rank judicial temperament highly, meaning whether the prospective justice would be a good colleague. In choosing among the other characteristics, they might each favor the ones that they happen to possess in abundance. Politicians might well see more merit in political savvy than would, say, academics, who could be expected to favor brains, the ability to abstract, and perhaps rhetorical skills.

All of these relevant actors might be honestly trying to come up with appropriate standards for measuring merit, but they would arrive at markedly different results. And any given result would screen out people who would succeed under another, equally plausible set of standards. Thus, if there is a genuine commitment to merit-based decision making it is possible that merit will out, but only for those who have the right kind of merit.

Which brings us to the prior question: is merit all we care about in deciding who gets what share of life's goodies? Clearly not. Does anyone, for example, honestly believe that any Supreme Court justice in recent memory was nominated solely on the basis of merit (however defined)? Any President? Any member of Congress? Does anyone believe that America's health-care resources are distributed solely on merit? That tax breaks are distributed solely on merit? That baseball club owners are selected solely on merit?

As I suggested earlier, the mere fact that a myth is based on false premises or conveys a false image of the world does not necessarily make it undesirable. Indeed, I place great stock in the idea that some illusions are, or at least can be, positive. As social psychologist Shelley Taylor has observed, "[normal] people who are confronted with the normal rebuffs of everyday life seem to construe their experience [so] as to develop and maintain an exaggeratedly positive view of their own attributes, an unrealistic optimism about the future, and a distorted faith in their ability to control what goes on around them."[4] Taylor's research suggests that, up to a point, such self-aggrandizement actually improves ones chances of worldly success.[5]

This may well explain the deep appeal of the Horatio Alger myth. True or not, it can help to pull people in the direction they want to go. After all, in order to succeed in life, especially when the odds are stacked against you, it is often necessary to first convince yourself that there is a reason to get up in the morning. So what is my beef? Where is the harm?

In a nutshell, my objection to the Alger myth is that it serves to maintain the racial pecking order. It does so by mentally bypassing the role of race in American society. And it does so by fostering beliefs that themselves serve to trivialize, if not erase, the social meaning of race. The Alger myth encourages people to blink at the many barriers to racial equality (historical, structural, and institutional) that litter the social landscape. Yes, slavery was built on the notion that Africans were property and not persons; yes, even after that "peculiar institution" collapsed, it continued to shape the life prospects of those who previously were enslaved; yes, the enforced illiteracy and cultural disruption of slavery, together with the collapse of Reconstruction, virtually assured that the vast majority of "freedmen" and "freedwomen" would not be successfully integrated into society; yes, Jim Crow laws, segregation, and a separate and unequal social reality severely undermined the prospects for Black achievement; yes, these and other features of our national life created a racial caste system that persists to this day; yes, the short-lived civil rights era of the 1950s and 1960s was undone by a broad and sustained White backlash; yes, the majority of Black people in America are mired in poverty; yes, economic mobility is not what it used to be, given the decline in our manufacturing and industrial base; yes, the siting of the illicit drug industry in our inner cities has had pernicious effects on Black and Latino neighborhoods; yes, yes, yes, BUT (drumroll) "all it takes to make it in America is initiative, hard work, persistence, and pluck." After all, just look at Colin Powell!

There is a fundamental tension between the promise of opportunity enshrined in the Alger myth and the realities of a racial caste system. The main point of such a system is to promote and maintain inequality. The main point of the Alger myth is to proclaim that everyone can rise above her station in life. Despite this tension, it is possible for the myth to coexist with social reality. To quote Shelley Taylor once again:

> [T]he normal human mind is oriented toward mental health and . . . at every turn it construes events in a manner that promotes benign fictions about the self, the world,

and the future. The mind is, with some significant exceptions, intrinsically adaptive, oriented toward overcoming
rather than succumbing to the adverse events of life. . . .
At one level, it constructs beneficent interpretations of
threatening events that raise self-esteem and promote moti-
vation; yet at another level, it recognizes the threat or challenge that is posed by these events.[6]

Not surprisingly, then, there are lots of Black folk who
subscribe to the Alger myth and at the same time understand
it to be deeply false. They live with the dissonance between
myth and reality because both are helpful and healthful in
dealing with "the adverse events of life." Many Whites, however, have a strong interest in resolving the dissonance in favor
of the myth. Far from needing to be on guard against racial
"threat[s] or challenge[s]," they would just as soon put the
ugliness of racism out of mind. For them, the Horatio Alger
myth provides them the opportunity to do just that.[7]

Quite apart from the general way in which the myth
works to submerge the social realities of race, each of the
messages it projects is also incompatible with the idea of race-
based advantage or disadvantage. If, as the myth suggests, we
are judged solely on our individual merits, then caste has little
practical meaning. If we all can acquire the tools needed to
reach our full potential, then how important can the disadvantage of race be? If merit will eventually carry the day, then
shouldn't we be directing our energies toward encouraging
Black initiative and follow-through rather than worrying
about questions of power and privilege?

By interring the myth of Horatio Alger, or at least forc-
ing it to coexist with social reality, we can accomplish two

important goals. First, we can give the lie to the idea that Black people can simply lift themselves up by their own bootstraps. With that pesky idea out of the way, it is easier to see why White folk need to take joint ownership of the nation's race problem. Second, the realization that hard work and individual merit, while certainly critical, are not guarantors of success should lead at least some White people to reflect on whether their own achievements have been helped along by their preferred social position.

Finally, quite apart from race, it is in our national interest to give the Horatio Alger myth a rest, for it broadcasts a fourth message no less false than the first three—that we live in a land of unlimited potential. Although that belief may have served us well in the past, we live today in an era of diminished possibilities. We need to make a series of hard choices, followed by yet more hard choices regarding how to live with the promise of less. Confronting that reality is made that much harder by a mythology that assures us we can have it all.

RESISTING TEMPTATION

Divide and conquer. It is one of the oldest tricks in the book. Armies use it to perfection. So do parents, coyotes, and cutting horses. It's a fine tactic if your cause is just. But when used to perpetuate the racial pecking order, it smacks of dirty pool.

Doubtless there are politicians, editorial writers, senior research fellows, and a Supreme Court justice or two who consciously seek to divide people of color along lines of race, class, politics, and culture. They are forever instigating: pitting the interests of one group against those of another; exalting leaders who are weak and tearing down those who are strong; spotlighting worrisome fissures and transforming them into gaping chasms. Their goal in all this is to keep people of color from coalescing and mounting a serious challenge to the existing order.

Many garden-variety White folk act in similar ways. I am convinced, however, that for them the process is far from conscious. And instead of being fueled by a straightforward desire to preserve power and privilege, it is fed by a desire to avoid being made to feel like a bad guy.

A standard move by Whites of all stripes is to pit successful people of color against less successful ones. For example, the educational and economic achievements of Asian-American immigrants are regularly trotted out as evidence of what can be accomplished despite racism. The implication is that the relatively poor showing of African-Americans must be attributable to defects in their own culture rather than to the behavior of Whites. The favorable comparison of Asian-Americans encourages them to distance themselves from the plight of African-Americans, and encourages African-Americans to turn on Asians. Not bad for a single day's work. But even if the comparison is simply whispered among friends behind closed doors rather than presented as a direct challenge to Black folk, it serves the purpose of allowing Whites to feel let off the hook.

This gambit works only if you ignore the true circumstances in which Asian-Americans find themselves. One can, of course, point to Asian-American success stories. But there are also Asian-American immigrants, including males from Korea, Vietnam, and the Philippines, who are economically no better off on average than African-Americans.[1] According to 1990 census data, nearly half of Southeast Asian immigrants live in poverty with annual income below ten thousand dollars.[2] Moreover, many of the success stories rely on incomplete or misleading data. For example, comparisons of median family income do not take account of the fact that immigrants from Japan, China, and Korea have more workers per family than do African-Americans (or Whites, for that matter).[3] Nor do they control for the fact that Asian-Americans are clustered in large metropolitan areas (more than half of all Asian-Americans live in Honolulu, San Francisco, Los Angeles, Chicago, or New York City[4]) that boast both high salaries and high costs of living.

Moreover, it is a mistake to assume that Asian-Americans who have succeeded economically have thereby been exempted from racism. Ask anyone who has been shunted into a particular job category or denied admission to an elite school based solely on her Asian appearance and name. Racism can be manifested in any number of ways. Indeed, if African-Americans had arrived on these shores with skills very much prized in a postindustrial economy, our economic status would be very different than it is today even if our place in the pecking order remained the same. Similarly, Asian-Americans, in particular Chinese men, who came to America during the Industrial Age were pressed into service as physical laborers and were consigned to the bottom of the economic heap. Therefore, differences in economic status between races or ethnic groups tell us very little, in and of themselves, about how race operates in America.

Touting Asian-Americans as a "model minority" also fails to control for the effects of the United States' immigration policy. Until 1976, the law gave preference to immigrants who were highly educated and highly skilled. Even though that preference has been repealed, the law's family reunification provisions continue to give preference to the relatives of folk who are already here. Therefore, to the extent that the various members of a family occupy the same social and economic class, the reunification provisions tend to perpetuate the effects of the pre-1976 preference for professionals. Immigration policy to the side, we should not be surprised at the fact that, in the absence of a major social upheaval, those who come to the United States from halfway around the world tend to be disproportionately drawn from the upper echelons of their native countries. To take just one example, the vast majority of India's population lacks the resources to even make it to the airport in Delhi or Bombay, much less arrive at JFK ready to take the United States by storm. Therefore, to compare struggling inner-city Blacks with Indian physicians, academics, and merchants is like comparing Calcutta's masses with the African-American elite.

Not only does the bandying about of the "model-minority myth" work to keep African-Americans in their place and to sow dissension between them and Asian-Americans. It tends to keep Asian-Americans in their place as well. After all, if they are being held out as a model, how can they complain? Praise of the sort accorded Asian-Americans these days is like a construction worker's (or law professor's) wolf whistle; it may be thought of as flattering by the giver and perhaps even the receiver, but in fact it is a means of expressing and reinforcing dominance. In exchange for not being denigrated (literally, treated like a Black person), Asian-Americans are treated as if they were White America's strange and exotic pet.

Divide and conquer has other uses besides fostering dissension among people of color. It can also create havoc within a single race. The most familiar form of it is a game that I call "Disavow That Leader." Although usually limited to one round, it can go on for several turns. Remember Jesse Jackson's 1984 presidential campaign? At stop after stop, Reverend Jackson was called upon to disavow Minister Farrakhan.[5] The implication was that if he did not, he could not be taken seriously as a candidate. At a minimum, he could forget about getting his own message across. Then, after Jackson began to display unexpectedly broad support in places like Iowa and Wisconsin, the Democratic Party was urged to disavow *him*.[6]

More recently, Assistant Attorney General Deval Patrick was repeatedly asked to distance himself from Lani Guinier as a condition of being confirmed as head of the Civil Rights Division.[7] She, of course, had previously been asked to distance herself from her own views and convictions.[8] The same thing happens on the local level, and not just in the political arena. It happens in churches, in workplaces, in civic organizations, and in academic settings. When Blacks appeal to Whites for help, too often they are asked to first affirm that they are not like the Black bogeyman of the moment.

Such "requests" are deeply unsettling. They smack of an attempt to control what gets said, to control who gets to say it, to divide loyalties, and to ensure that the Black community's leaders are tractable. They are also profoundly insulting. They assume that Black people are all of one mind unless we publicly declare to the contrary; that we are incapable of recognizing and rejecting harmful messages without the guidance of a White overlord; that we pick our leaders for their least attractive qualities rather than for their strengths; and that in any event our judgments of people, pro or con, are irrelevant. I would voluntarily take many a Black person to task for spewing invective and spreading a politics of hate— Khalid Abdul Muhammad comes readily to mind—but I'll be damned if I will do so in response to White folk who want to see me dance on a string.

A second way that *intra*racial discord is fostered is by taking a simmering Black-on-Black conflict and turning up the heat. Recently I received a large envelope in the mail from a law professor who was unknown to me. That is not unusual; I receive unsolicited law review articles seemingly every other day. But this was different. Instead of an article, the envelope contained copies of a newspaper clipping and several memos to the file. At first I thought I had been sent the packet by mistake, but on closer inspection I put it all together. The sender, it seems, is a tenured Black professor who, in the context of the possible appointment of a second Black woman to her school's faculty, had expressed views about the difference between skin color, race, and ethnicity. She apparently had questioned whether the candidate, the offspring of a White Australian mother and a Black Cuban father, should be considered "Black" for purposes of demonstrating racial diversity. Noting that there are several ways to define race in the American context, the professor argued that "Black" should be restricted to "those descended from U.S. slaves."

Despite the fact that the candidate had withdrawn herself from consideration, an account of the professor's statements to the faculty had been leaked to the local press. By the time she sent me the bundle of memos, the story had already been picked up by *The New Republic,* and *The Wall Street Journal* had run an editorial. More press was in the offing from, among other places, the New York *Times,* and she wrote to communicate her side of the story to Black professors who might well be asked to opine on the controversy. I logged onto Lexis/Nexis to see what the press had to say, and was amazed to discover that the word had stretched from Sacramento to Boston and that the coverage had lasted a full three months. Virtually without exception, the news stories had a kind of leering, drooling quality and were heavy on the sarcasm. The reporters all lined up on the side of the candidate, but it struck me that they didn't care about her so much as they hungered to present a picture of one Black person victimizing another.

So where does all this leave us? For those who are intent on perpetuating America's racial hierarchy for as long as possible, there are obviously short-term gains to be reaped from playing divide and conquer. To them I have little to say, and I doubt that they have read this far. But for the majority of White folk who lapse into a divisive mode without thinking, and who do so for no better (and no worse) reason than to deflect attention from themselves, a bit of self-consciousness and self-restraint is in order. Setting others to fighting is a classic way of avoiding the responsibility to take joint ownership of America's race problem.

As for the view that Black people "need to think about" the fact that other minorities have managed to do well for themselves, or that not all Blacks are on the same page, I question the messenger more than the message. We do need to consider whether there are lessons to be learned from the experiences of Asian-Americans, Arab-Americans, and others who have achieved a measure of economic success in the teeth of racism and bigotry. But we need to look at the real deal, and not the filtered, distorted, and truncated version that serves the interests of White folk with a point to make. And as far as our internal divisions are concerned, to the extent that disruptive or even destructive forces exist within the Black community, we are, I assure you, well aware of them. No good will come from having White knights ride to the rescue. All we will be able to hear is the sound of their barely suppressed glee. Perhaps our reaction will be misplaced, but what consolation is that?

PART FOUR

What Black Folk Must Do

RETELL THE STORY

There is a view abroad in the land that most Black folk are stuck in the past; that we have thoroughly embraced a vision of ourselves as victims and are loath to take responsibility for our own circumstances or to acknowledge progress; that we use slavery, segregation, and discrimination as all-purpose excuses for our own failings; that we are caught up in playing the "blame game," thereby alienating our allies and leaving our enemies unscathed; and that in any event it is high time for us to give it a rest and move on. Although well-meaning Whites rarely express this "victimization thesis" in our presence except in the most muted of tones, friends assure me that behind closed doors such sentiments are freely expressed and broadly held.

Within the Black community, reactions to this indictment vary. Some folk are so mesmerized by the elements of truth in it that they fail to exercise any critical judgment whatsoever.[1] Others, like Stanley Crouch and Robert Woodson, have seized upon it as an opportunity to trumpet the value of self-help, a theme that has reverberated throughout our history.[2] Still others, myself included, worry that White America's rush to embrace this new received wisdom is not a good thing. The victimization thesis renders our historical mistreatment invisible. It is a respectable way of saying, "That is old news." While ostensibly a claim about our present state of mind (which is presumptuous enough, especially when it comes from folk who have never tried to really know us), ultimately the thesis calls into question the extent of the harm done to us in the first place. Just maybe, reads the subtext, we really don't have anything to complain about.

The victimization thesis is, to be blunt, a perfect example of racism in action. Not bigotry; racism—the embracing of attitudes and beliefs that allow those who sit atop the racial hierarchy to do so in relative comfort. By focusing on Black people's psychology, otherwise thoughtful White people distance themselves from our plight, lessen any guilt they feel with respect to past depredations, and avoid having to deal with the fact that they continue to be racially advantaged.

They do not embrace the victimization thesis out of malice or a conscious desire to maintain the racial hierarchy. They don't even consciously seek to walk away from America's race problem. They simply want to avoid feeling like bad guys. It's really quite simple. If Black people are not really victims, then White people are not really victimizers. Unfortunately, the price of their relief is more pain for us.

Unfortunately, the victimization thesis has taken wing just as our society has had its fill of people who seek to justify criminal behavior on the grounds that it was precipitated by a pattern of abuse. Depending on your taste in these matters, the high-water mark was either the Lorena Bobbitt trial (in which the defendant sought to escape responsibility for severing her husband's penis) or the Menendez trial (in which defendants sought to reduce the penalty for killing their parents). Similarly, discontent grew in the 1990s over what many regard as a growing tendency on the part of Americans to attribute personal failures to forces beyond their control. In an especially funny episode, one of the characters on television's *Designing Women* insisted that she could not be held accountable for her insufferable behavior because she suffered from OPD, obnoxious personality disorder. The tenor of the times is reflected in the title of a 1994 book by Alan Dershowitz: *The Abuse Excuse: Cop-outs, Sob Stories, and Other Evasions of Responsibility.*[3]

In this environment, it is increasingly difficult to speak of the evils of the past, or even of the wrongdoings of the present, without producing a fishy-eyed stare. Nevertheless, it is important that Black folk not give up on trying to tell our story as best we can. In order to change the way things are, we first have to understand how they came to be. Treating effects without understanding their causes can be dangerous and even life-threatening. In addition, we need to lay out the record of our—dare I use the word?—victimization in order to free ourselves from it. Before we can reframe it, we must first name it. It is also important that the wrong done to us be acknowledged in some way. For as anyone who has been in a relationship can testify, it is crazy-making to feel aggrieved and to have those grievances be discounted or trivialized. At best, such withholding adds insult to injury.

At the same time, we need to admit that, just as with

any other genuine pattern of abuse, there are some people who become locked in the role of victim and others who consciously use it for their own ends. We need to learn how to distinguish between wallowers, scam artists, and the great mass of Black folk who would love nothing better than to put their victimization behind them. Too often, we have simply walked away from sisters and brothers who are stuck—who believe almost literally that "The White man has his foot on my neck"—and have winked at those who are just trying to get over. We need to somehow reach out to the former and rein in the latter, all the while insisting that the entire Black community should not be painted in either of their images.

For most of us Black folk, the problem is not that we are mired in victimhood; it is that we no longer are able to give a satisfactory account of who we are and why we remain on the bottom. The story we are accustomed to telling is incomplete, overly simplistic, and badly out of date. It fails to connect the past to the present, and does not address the great variability in our experiences. Too often, we don't even tell the standard story well, lapsing into indecipherable shorthand or substituting invective for explanation.

The standard story goes something like this.

We were brought to this continent in chains, physically enslaved, deprived of all freedom, and subjected to continuous abuse. Our culture was suppressed, our families ripped apart, and our women raped. We were deliberately kept ignorant, and were prohibited from learning to read or write. Our attempts to rebel were brutally crushed. Despite all this, we survived as a people, developed a strong culture of resistance, and endured.

When we were eventually emancipated, we did not become truly free. Even our emancipators had no interest in embracing us as equals, and we lacked the knowledge and resources to create a world of our own. Our only choice was to remain subservient.

The era of Reconstruction—society's effort to help us get on our feet—was altogether too brief, and was followed by a long period of bondage by another name. Slavery was replaced by Black Codes and Jim Crow laws. The slavemaster's whip was replaced by the lynch mob's rope. Legal advances were often ephemeral, and were offset by grandfather clauses, literacy tests, and outright intimidation. "Separate but equal" was the law of the land, and somehow only the first part ever got enforced.

When legal segregation gave way in response to agitation from Black people and their White allies, de facto segregation took its place. It continues to this day in much of daily life. Once formal segregation was ended, the civil rights movement took on discrimination in employment, housing, and public accommodations. After a series of legislative and judicial victories, backlash and retrenchment set in. New barriers were erected. Suddenly, progress for us was seen as a form of "reverse discrimination." Meanwhile, those Blacks who did manage to enter the mainstream discovered that it was less than hospitable.

On a related front, we began in various ways to explore and assert our distinctive cultural identity. We looked to our African roots for inspiration in art, music, history, rituals, and even the names we give our children. We paid attention to our hybrid African-American culture,

and developed ways of giving it expression. We had
scarcely begun when a cultural backlash set in. In many
quarters, nationalism and multiculturalism came to be seen
as sinister, and as an attempt to impose political correct-
ness. Suddenly, White males were being hailed in the press
as America's true victims.

While we were struggling on all these fronts, the
economy underwent a sea change. Manufacturing jobs and
entry-level jobs in other fields with prospects for advance-
ment are nowhere to be found. Unskilled and semiskilled
jobs have fled overseas. Even as formal racial barriers come
down, we are stuck at the bottom with no place to go. In
many ways, Black men have become an endangered species.
With no way to provide for families by legitimate means,
the lure of easy money on the street, and the availability of
addictive substances to dull the pain, we risk losing an
entire generation to the nation's prisons and jails, to drugs,
and to AIDS.

This narrative is quite compelling, and is a powerful
reminder of the difficult road we have traveled together as a
people. However, as an explanation for why our community
continues to suffer so, it is much too tidy. It glosses over those
aspects of our experience that might rob us of sympathy or
make our current predicament seem less inevitable. And it
raises almost as many questions as it answers. We must, for
example, acknowledge that the path from slavery to the present has not been a straight one, and that much has happened
in recent years that cries out for explanation. We cannot afford
to leave troubling details uncommented upon, for when we
tell our story to others we tell it to ourselves as well. We owe
it to ourselves to understand our lives in all their complexity.

As for potential detractors, better to disarm them with candor and forethought than to give their misgivings free rein to roam.

Specifically, the standard story does not deal adequately with the following awkward realities.

1. Although slavery was undeniably awful, it ended several generations ago. How could it possibly have any bearing on the way things are today? And is it fair to blame people today for the sins of their great-grandparents? Also, what about all those people (Black as well as White) who immigrated to the United States *after* slavery?

2. Prior generations of African-Americans had many fewer opportunities and encountered much more virulent bigotry and discrimination, yet they somehow managed to survive intact. Why, then, are so many of us having such a tough time of it?

3. At the other extreme, there are lots of very successful Black folk running around. How have they managed to make it? Apart from individual success stories, hasn't considerable progress been made on the institutional level? Look at our gains in the political arena, in the arts, in mass media. Even in the corporate and academic worlds, our presence is small but growing. Meanwhile, raw bigotry is out of fashion and potential allies are everywhere. Is racism less of a barrier than we think?

4. Does it make sense to even talk about a Black community? After all, we are far from monolithic. What sense does it make to speak as if we are all in the same boat when some of us are worried about the corporate glass ceiling while others are looking for a benefits floor to support them? Can we even claim to have a common political vision anymore?

5. Other racial minorities, in particular Asian-Americans, seem to be making a pretty good go of it. If they can make it, why can't we?

6. Are our detractors correct in claiming that our continued marginality stems from the fact that we have abandoned the Protestant ethic and have substituted in its place self-destructive values and behavior patterns? If not, how do we account for the moral chaos of the inner city?

These difficulties are far from trivial. We need to address them head-on. Although they are sometimes posed in a hostile manner, or with the intention of putting us at a disadvantage, we cannot afford to treat them solely as trick questions. What is more, we need to get our act together soon, so that we do not continue ceding to others the power to frame the debate. By the time we are feeling brave enough or desperate enough to join in, it may be too late.

My goal in these pages is to promote a lively and productive debate within the Black community around these issues. I don't pretend to have any well-formed answers, but I do have some preliminary thoughts, starting with the contemporary relevance of slavery. One thing seems clear: we need to be more careful in the way we talk about it, and more attentive to the take-home message we wish to convey. When we simply describe the horrors of slavery and leave to our audience the task of drawing the moral, we fairly invite a dismissive response. After all, isn't such cruelty unthinkable in the waning days of the twentieth century? Haven't we, therefore, closed the book on that ignominious chapter of our history?

The flaw in this reasoning is well captured by William Styron, author of *The Confessions of Nat Turner*,[4] in an Op-Ed piece critiquing the Disney Corporation's now abandoned plan to include slavery exhibits in a northern Virginia theme park. A Disney spokesperson had said that the exhibits would make visitors "feel what it was like to be a slave, and what it was like to escape through the Underground Railroad."[5] But, says Styron:

> [N]o combination of branding irons, slave ships or slave cabins, shackles, chained black people in their wretched coffles, or treks through the Underground Railroad could begin to define such a stupendous experience. To present even the most squalid sights would be to cheaply romanticize suffering.
>
> For slavery's abysmal pain arose far less from its physical cruelty—although slave ships and the auction block were atrocities—than from the moral and legal savagery that deprived an entire people of their freedom, along with their rights to education, ownership of property, matrimony and protection under the law.[6]

By mindlessly focusing on slavery's physical cruelty, we, like the Disney Corporation if it had its way, entice White people into a false catharsis. We permit them, with "a shudder of horror," to "turn away, smug and exculpatory, from a world" they wrongly believe to have been "laid to rest."[7]

Our task, therefore, is to retell the slavery narrative in a way that makes it less of a history lesson and more of a present reality. The key is to be explicit about the ways in which slavery lives on in our lives. Professor D. Marvin Jones has highlighted an important one. Slavery has enduring significance, he explains, not because of the monstrous but transitory harms done to those who were enslaved, but rather because it served to indelibly link Blackness and subservience in the American subconscious. At a deep level, slavery stamped Black people as inferior, as lacking in virtue, as lacking the capacity to order their own lives. In addition, the literal as well as metaphorical dehumanization of captive Africans made it possible for White Americans to resolve the contradiction between their professed commitment to freedom and their subjugation of other human beings. If the Africans weren't really human, then there was no contradiction. The depredations of slavery helped to cement this idea: "If Blacks are seen to be treated as animals, this confirms that they are animals."[8]

Thus, slavery continues to shape our lives more than a century after abolition because the link it forged between Blackness and inferiority, Blackness and subservience, Blackness and danger, has survived to this day. Slavery's enduring legacy is that our "subhumanity" has been deeply imprinted in the American psyche. The resulting mental imprint continues to shape the way people think about race to this very day. It does not matter that contemporary Black folk were not personally enslaved so long as we carry the stigmata of those who were—dark skin. Similarly, it does not matter whether our White counterparts actually descended from slavemasters so long as they inherited from our culture the mind-set that made it possible for liberty-loving, God-fearing people to subordinate their fellow human beings.

The imprint of slavery—Blackness equals mental weakness, moral looseness, physical aggressiveness, sexual uninhibitedness, and general beastliness—has found contemporary expression in the way in which Rodney King was described by the police officers who used him for batting practice. He was "bearlike," "hulklike," and "like a wounded animal."[9] One of the officers described an earlier encounter with Black people as like *Gorillas in the Mist.*[10] Black people's awareness of this phenomenon helps explain our deep apprehension regarding the criminal trials of Mike Tyson and O. J. Simpson, and the confirmation hearings of Clarence Thomas, without regard for whether we thought them guilty or innocent, fit or unfit to serve.[11] It also helps explain our visceral negative response to the efforts by some epidemiologists to trace the origins of the AIDS virus (HIV) to Africa and in particular to a similar retrovirus found in the green monkey.[12] And it helps to explain Isiah Thomas's publicly expressed irritation (for which he was severely chastised by the sports establishment) over the tendency of commentators to compare Black basketball players to "animals, lions and tigers who run around the jungle."[13] The same commentators attribute Black players' success to "God-given talent" while attributing White players' success to "thinking," "work habits," and "intelligence."[14]

Therefore, in retelling our story we need to describe more precisely how slavery lives on in our lives; not as broken bones or clanking chains, but as a largely unconscious way of framing how we are seen, how we see ourselves, and how we relate to the world around us. We also need to speak to the puzzling fact that even though our forebears lived in a much harsher world insofar as race is concerned, they managed to thrive as a community as compared to many Black communities today. This unexpected inversion has led a lot of White people and more than a few Blacks to quite reasonably ask whether we contemporary Black folk are somehow undermining ourselves. Perhaps we are doing something wrong that we used to do right.

Filling in this part of our story is tricky, because it

means describing the many ways in which integration has worked to our disadvantage. Or, to put it more starkly, it means acknowledging that segregation was beneficial to us in certain ways. That doesn't mean, of course, that on balance segregation was like a Sunday at the beach, nor does it mean that there is no third way that would combine the advantages of the old and the new. In a nutshell, strict boundaries made it both necessary and possible for Black people to "have each other's back." We were all in the same boat, physically, economically, and spiritually. We were a community in the deepest sense of the word. We raised each other's children, policed our own neighborhoods, and focused on making our own institutions strong.

We were much more economically interdependent than today. Businessmen and businesswomen could not succeed without the patronage and support of an intact Black community. But then again, Black consumers were not welcome in the downtown stores anyway. Black professionals had no choice but to serve their own. Attorneys, for example, did not have the option of working for a law firm outside the neighborhood or for the city attorney or state attorney general. Physicians did not receive offers from HMOs or from private practices that saw White patients. People like me weren't teaching in predominantly White universities a generation or two ago. We were more likely to be found in all-Black colleges, high schools, and grade schools, ensuring that the next generation was twice as prepared as would be necessary if life were fair. Thus, although our forebears faced much more menacing demons than do we, they were better girded for battle in many ways and they did not fight alone.

Strict segregation produced other advantages as well. Black people were much more likely to be aware of their own culture and to draw on and enrich it as a matter of course. We were much more likely to enter into robust political debate, secure that we could keep arguments within the family and not have to worry that what we said would be exploited by people who didn't have our best interests at heart. And in a curious sort of way, we had much greater faith that things would get better, in part because every way was up, but also because we were taking on naked evil rather than well-dressed power.

Finally, in some ways Black people are worse off today. In addition to the exquisite difficulty of dealing with an "enemy" that is diffuse, friendly, and mostly well-meaning, we face many roadblocks that are only partially related to race. For example, today's economy is much less penetrable than at any other time in America's history. This is a problem that knows no color, but to the extent that Black folk are especially unlikely to possess the skills and experience needed to make it in a twenty-first-century economy, we as a community are particularly disadvantaged. We also have to deal with what has been termed the "crisis of rising expectations." It is a well-documented aspect of human psychology that once an unsatisfactory situation begins to improve, it is much more difficult to adjust to setbacks or even a lack of forward progress than if there had been no improvement in the first place.[15] Then there is the challenge of trying to preserve "family" values (i.e., those that have sustained the African-American family for generations) at a time when the mass culture touts instant gratification and measures success by what you

wear, drive, or consume. Finally, the emergence of crack co-
caine has crippled the Black inner city in ways that we are just
beginning to fully comprehend.[16]

After filling in why so many of us continue to struggle
more than might have been predicted, we need to flip the coin
over and deal with the fact that American society has made
vast strides in recent decades. We should acknowledge that
significant progress has indeed been made. To do otherwise is
to deny our own hard work, as well as to appear either unnecessarily grudging or woefully out of touch. But we also need
to highlight in very specific and concrete terms what has *not*
changed for the better.

We need to point out, for example, that the gap between
Black and White infant mortality has persisted, and indeed
gotten worse, since 1950;[17] that the gap between Black and
White median family income has gotten worse since 1970,
with Black families today earning just 54 percent of what
White families do;[18] that the unemployment gap has remained unchanged during the same period, with the rate for
Blacks being twice that for Whites;[19] that among the employed, Blacks earn significantly less than comparably educated Whites at every level.[20] The effect on the young is especially noteworthy. Nearly half of Black children live in
poverty, compared to less than 13 percent of White children.[21]

Nor is equal opportunity necessarily a reality for those
who are in a position to take advantage of it. For the moment,
two examples should suffice. It is twice as difficult for Blacks
to obtain mortgages as Whites with comparable income, according to a recent Federal Reserve study.[22] And it is three
times as difficult for Blacks to obtain employment in the ser-

vice sector, according to studies involving carefully matched pairs of job seekers.[23] Through this kind of careful marshaling of the evidence, we can demonstrate—rather than just assert —that even in the face of palpable progress, the basic structure of America's racial hierarchy remains unchanged.

As for the fact that some Black folk seem to be doing quite well, that too is undeniable. However, once again we should press the inquiry a step further. To what extent are Black success stories attributable to progress in race relations? To a considerable extent, the Black community has been the mother of its own good fortune. Thus, several of the top twenty Black-owned industrial and service corporations (measured by sales) are in the business of producing Black-oriented media. Two companies in the top twenty and five in the top fifty manufacture cosmetics and hair products aimed at a Black market.[24] At the same time, a rapidly expanding segment of the most successful Black businesses cater to a much broader clientele. That sounds like progress. Still, one has to wonder whether someone like J. Bruce Llewellyn, the owner of two companies in the *Black Enterprise* top ten, or William Gray, the former Democratic whip of the House of Representatives, would have been even more successful if his skin were white.

If we move down a notch or two from the comfortably wealthy to the merely comfortable, we ought to readily acknowledge the rapid rise of a Black professional and managerial class. At the same time, we should point out that the success of its members is easily overstated. In *The Rage of a Privileged Class,* Ellis Cose illustrates poignantly the diminished status many of them occupy in the workplace. Racism, it seems, knows no class lines. This phenomenon is not much

talked about because "society . . . does not want to hear
that privileged members of a generally 'underprivileged'
group still harbor serious complaints."[25]

In addition to the sense that they are somehow on a
separate track, Cose sets out what he calls the "dozen demons"
that plague the Black middle class: the inability to fit in;
exclusion from the club; low expectations; shattered hopes;
faint praise; presumption of failure; coping fatigue; pigeonhol-
ing; self-censorship and silence; mendacity; identity problems;
and guilt by association.[26] From my own experience, I would
add three more. The first is a variation on survivor's guilt.
When I became a lawyer, my father asked me how much I was
making. I tried to finesse the question, but eventually gave in.
Every time I switched jobs he asked the same question, and
each time I answered with great reluctance. I knew that
Daddy wanted to assure himself that I was doing well and to
bask in reflected success, but for me those occasions were painful reminders that I was blessed with opportunities no one else
in my family could even dream of. I still am unable to comfortably accept the fact that I make more money in a year than
my father could in several, or that if I were to sign on with a
fancy law firm my annual partnership share would exceed my
parents' joint income for a decade or more.

I have a related fear of becoming detached from my
roots. Some years ago I wrote the following, which pretty well
captures the feeling. "The day that I am awarded tenure,
should that happy event occur, any pleasure that I experience
will be more than offset by the extreme panic that I'm sure
will set in[.] I will worry that I have . . . wittingly, selfishly
and self-destructively propelled myself two steps further away

from so much that has nurtured me for so long."[27] After
tenure, I simply reattached the worry to something else. My
third demon is that from time to time I am trotted out by
White folk as a kind of "racial-progress poster boy." While I
suppose this comes with the territory, that is precisely my
point. The territory of Black success is not all that it is
cracked up to be. Obviously, most Black folk would gladly
switch places with me or with the people profiled in Cose's
book, but for White folk in comparable positions, trading
places wouldn't be much fun.

As for the claim that the Black community is not monolithic, once again we should feel no embarrassment about acknowledging its force. Indeed, we should celebrate our differences and advertise our great variety. Name a point of view
and we can probably find some Black folk who embrace it.
Describe an interest and there are Black folk who share it. The
mere fact that we are heterogeneous does not mean that there
is no such thing as the Black community. It does, however,
oblige us to articulate what makes us a community—what we
have in common that transcends our many differences. Lots of
us *feel* a sense of common purpose, feel it in our bones, but it
is high time we commanded our bones to speak.

Similarly, the fact that we are not monolithic does not
mean that it is impossible to speak about what the Black
community needs, wants, or believes. Americans are not
monolithic, yet people think nothing of talking about
quintessentially "American" values, ideals, and aspirations.
Southerners, military brass, Minnesotans, suburbanites, teenagers, Evangelical Christians, and power lifters are not monolithic, yet we manage to say useful things about each of them

as a group. We also manage to distinguish between characterizations that are accurate enough and those that are overblown or off the mark. Of course, in every group there are dissenters. There are indeed military officers with a bit of the rebel in them, Minnesotans who are not nice, and Americans who do not like apple pie. But that does not mean that there is no rule against which exceptions can be measured. One of the great advantages of owning up to our heterogeneity is that doing so frees us to make useful distinctions. We should not pretend that people like Thomas Sowell and Walter Williams do not exist, but we can surely demonstrate that they are not broadly representative of the Black community.

When asked to account for the fact that Asian-Americans (and in some cities Latinos) seem to be doing much better than Blacks, at least economically, we tend to lapse into near-silence. We do manage to retort that they weren't brought here in chains, but the significance of that distinction is often lost on others because of our failure to specify why the experience of slavery continues to matter. Our attempts to articulate a theory of color preference—the darker the skin, the tougher the sledding—are brought up short by the fact that many successful immigrants from the Indian subcontinent are considerably darker than many less successful African-Americans.

Our answers fall short largely because we haven't really paid much attention to the background, distinctive history, and social reality of other people of color. Mostly, we have viewed them through the lens of our own experiences. We really haven't thought much about the ways in which their interactions with Whites differ from our own, or about how they may have coped with problems that seemed to us insurmountable. In order to retell this particular part of our story, we need to go back to school. The more we learn about the lived reality of our sisters and brothers of color, the more we will be able to resist efforts to play one group off against another.

With a bit of effort, we can cease viewing Asian-Americans as one indistinct mass. We can learn to differentiate between, say, Hmong living in squalor in Minnesota and Sansei (third-generation Japanese-Americans) living comfortably in the suburbs of California; between Filipino cabdrivers and Chinese-American businessmen who profit richly from Pacific Rim trade. We can isolate the role that immigration laws play in the overall Asian-American success story, especially the strong preferences they give to the highly skilled and well-educated. We can begin to ask different questions, such as whether Asian-American immigrants are able to compete with White Americans on terms of equality in their chosen professions, or are instead forced to climb down the occupational ladder in order to make a go of it. We can ask whether their sons and daughters are allowed to compete on terms of equality, given the skills that they have developed. We can ask a set of questions about assimilation, including: the different desires different groups form about whether to assimilate, given their historic relationships with America; the capacity of different groups to assimilate; and the particular risks each faces from assimilation, cultural as well as social. In short, by doing our homework we can transform a pretend conversation that seeks to simplify the impact of race in America into a full-scale dialogue that reveals the utter complexity, variability, and adaptability of racism.

Finally, let me say a few words about the observation

that in city after city across the country, Black people, especially the young, seem to have adopted value systems and behavior patterns that are harmful to them and to the community as well. At the risk of sounding like a broken record, I think that we should acknowledge the force of this claim too. We might want to quibble around the edges, and to quarrel seriously with the uses to which the claim is put, but we ought not deny that something has gone radically wrong in the neighborhood. At the same time, we should stress what a profound change this is for a people that historically has embraced the Protestant ethic and the Golden Rule with a vengeance. And we should ask the following questions: Did we develop these pathologies on our own? Did our young just wake up one morning no longer believing in the future, bereft of hope, and convinced that their lives do not matter? Is this simply a case of bad genes kicking in? Or is there some broader, more societal explanation for this sea change?

The short answer is that the Black community's deepening nihilism (to borrow Cornel West's favorite term) has more than one parent. Black people did not create a welfare system that fosters dependency, undermines initiative, rewards failure, and drives away fathers. We did not ask industry to dry up, move to the suburbs, or ship jobs overseas. We did not ask White people to flee the cities and take their tax dollars with them. We did not ask suburbs to resist metropolitan solutions to metropolitan problems. We did not ask drug importers to set up distribution networks in our neighborhoods; to provide our young with quick cash and a "get out of jail free" card; to make our streets unsafe; or to provide our vulnerable with the easy opportunity to become addicts. We did not ask the National Rifle Association and its allies in Congress to do their level best to ensure that ten-year-olds could talk knowledgeably about 9 millimeter handguns, AK-47s, and Uzis, while knowing next to nothing about the metric system, Russia's economy, or Middle East peace talks. I don't hold the Black community blameless. We should have taken better care of ourselves and of our own. But there is an equally important truth that must be told: we did not slide into the abyss all by ourselves. And painful as it is to admit, we can't climb out of it without help.

As we face up to these ticklish issues, it is important that we incorporate our new accounts into the larger story rather than treat them as alternatives whole unto themselves. Too often when we finally deal with a hidden demon, we act as if all else is beside the point. Remember the news reports a while back about the failed attempt to integrate the former Ku Klux Klan stronghold of Vidor, Texas? In response to a court order, the county housing authority had recruited four Black families to integrate Vidor's public housing project. This led to a series of hostile rallies, a cross burning, bomb threats, and other forms of harassment. Thoroughly intimidated, the Black tenants moved out. The last to leave was Bill Simpson, who returned to his old Black neighborhood of Beaumont, Texas, only to be killed by two would-be robbers within twelve hours of escaping Vidor.[28]

Much ink was spilled over this tragic story, but an article headlined "We Have Met the Enemy . . ." caught my eye. Written by Courtland Milloy, a respected Black Washington *Post* reporter, it began by noting that in response to the efforts to intimidate Simpson and the others, 2,000 Black people had descended on Vidor to stage a counterdemonstration.

[However, when Simpson] was fatally shot by two black gunmen during a robbery[,] [n]obody protested that. Here was a classic race relations case for our times, complete with white bogymen who divert attention from the fundamental problem in black America: us, black people. The federal response to Simpson's death showed no sign of understanding this. Henry Cisneros, the secretary of housing and urban development, seized control of the all-white enclave last week and promised to move in a dozen new black families. He must believe that being close to white people is black folk's best hope. The problem, though, is not Vidor. It's the neighborhood where Simpson was killed. And, unfortunately, too many people are reluctant to hold black perpetrators accountable.[29]

I applaud Milloy for calling attention to the issue of accountability for Black-on-Black crime, but I resist the notion that "the fundamental problem in black America [is] black people." Similarly, it is misleading to state that "the problem . . . is not Vidor." Why must there be only one problem? Why must we choose between caring about discrimination in Vidor and crime in Beaumont? Aren't they related? Isn't the real tragedy that Bill Simpson had no decent choices?

In retelling our story, we need to do a much better job of articulating *all* of the ways in which race matters. We need to describe the effects of racism and discrimination on our daily lives. We need to describe its effect on our psyches. I still wince at the internalized self-hatred reflected in the ways we used to chide each other when I was growing up. Put-downs such as: "Niggers and flies. Niggers and flies. The more I see niggers, the more I like flies." And we need to describe the ways in which racism has been imprinted on our bodies, as we learn more and more about hypertension and other stress-related diseases that plague us disproportionately.[30] We need not describe ourselves as basket cases—most of us are going concerns—but we owe it to ourselves to fully describe the toll.

Finally, we need to rethink the story we tell about White folk as well as the one we tell about ourselves. Our standard approach has been to pin our troubles on Bad White People and invite Good White People to come to our rescue. However, as the BWP fade from the scene, it has become evident that the GWP are part of the problem as well. Our message has to be that condemning bigotry and decrying ignorance are not enough. We need to ask our White allies to explore the ways in which *they* are unwitting preservers of racism and undeserving beneficiaries of racial advantage. In effect, it means accusing our friends of racism (albeit of the soft, nonbigoted kind) and then asking them to respond with an open mind. That is asking a lot.

To ease the conversation, we should delete the term "racist" from our vocabulary. Like any well-worn word, it has many shades of meaning, but when used to describe people its dominant message is that they are poisonous of heart and determined to do wrong. Most people's insides are much more complex, muted, uncertain, and contradictory than that. Our current vocabulary doesn't allow us to speak about *them* very well. There are, to be sure, plenty of nasty hate-filled people in the world. But there are a lot more who are just trying to get by. And there are many White folk who are desperately trying to do the right thing even as they act in ways that keep us down.

My concern is that by using language that conjures up images of naked bigotry, we lose sight of the vast majority of decent White people and fail to recognize that they collectively are more responsible for preserving and entrenching the racial pecking order than are the relatively few jerks who spew venom or act out of hatred. If we target "racists" as the enemy, with all the gritty overtones and suggestions of malice that that label projects, we let most people off the hook. After all, they happily condemn David Duke and Jesse Helms and perhaps even think that Lani Guinier got a raw deal. On the other hand, if we attach the label "racist" to them as well, to people whose attitudes and beliefs are misconceived rather than malicious, the targets of our ire will feel justified in withdrawing from us and turning their backs on our concerns.

Deleting the term "racist" from our vocabulary would cause us to fumble and grope at first, but ultimately it would force us to focus on what White people do and say rather than on what is in their hearts. And it would force us to spell out in detail, for ourselves as well as for others, the ways in which "culturally acceptable" words and deeds keep us at the bottom.

PULL TOGETHER
AS THE COMMUNITY

"Have you heard about the new first-year?" On the opening day of the 1994–95 school year, the halls were abuzz. Three different students buttonholed me, eager to tell the same story. For several years running, BALSA (the Black law students' association) had assigned a "buddy" to each incoming Black student to provide support and counsel. Well, it seems that this time around one young woman had taken great offense at the offer. "What makes you think I need a buddy?" she reportedly had asked. "What makes you think I even want anything to do with BALSA?" The students were aghast, and I must admit that I too was a bit taken aback.

In my experience, Black folk usually feel a sense of kinship with one another, especially in settings where we are greatly outnumbered or our worthiness is in question. Usually, we see ourselves as joined in a common cause, and we recognize that our fates are intertwined. At a minimum, we like to believe that our sisters and brothers "have our back." It is not surprising, then, that we tend to think of ourselves as constituting a "community." Black folk who don't feel particularly connected to the community often experience the gap as a loss. In any event, they know better than to run around advertising their alienation.

The first-year law student's response was extremely off-putting, but the same sentiments are expressed these days with increasing frequency. The truth is that "the Black community" has ceased to feel like homeplace to a lot of Black folk. We have become badly fragmented, so much so that many thoughtful people believe that we should no longer speak of ourselves as a single community.[1] We are not as clear as we once were about what exactly we have in common.

The answers that have served us well for most of our history no longer seem quite so compelling. Our shared sense of oppression has, of course, been a powerful unifying force. Despite our various divisions, beginning on the plantation when we were separated into house hands and field hands, we have always known that "to a hammer everything looks like a nail."[2] Even in the midst of the high optimism of the civil rights movement, we thought of ourselves as equally apt to get pounded, despite the fact that some of us were shinier or sturdier than others. When someone asked, "What do you call a Black man with a Ph.D?" we already knew the answer— "nigger"—or at least we responded knowingly when it was revealed. Today, however, increasing numbers of Black folk are convinced that *they* have risen above it all and that their race does not constrain their lives in any appreciable way.

We also used to be bound together by a shared political vision. Early on, the goals were simple and straightforward. Abolition of slavery; meaningful reconstruction; repeal of the so-called Black Codes; an end to lynching. Even as recently as the 1950s, 1960s, and 1970s, we had a shared commitment to what some have termed the Second Reconstruction: ending segregation; securing a meaningful right to vote; equalizing access to quality education; equalizing and expanding employment opportunity. We had our differences, of course, over both goals and tactics, but for the most part Malcolm and Martin, Roy Wilkins and Stokely Carmichael, were opposite sides of the same coin.

These days, however, our political unity seems to be dissolving. That is a predictable consequence of the steady softening of discrimination and racism. Instead of having doors slammed in our faces, we are cordially invited to come on in. Instead of being denied an application, we are encouraged to fill one out. Instead of failing to make the first cut, we make it to the final round. And when the rejection letter finally arrives, it has a pretty bow tied around it. (Something like: "We were not able to make you an offer at this time, but we really enjoyed having the chance to get to know you.") Similarly, we hardly ever run into Bull Connor or even David Duke anymore. Instead, we encounter people who are ostensibly on our side and who seek to protect us from the stigma of affirmative action and the dependency created by too much government support. Instead of confronting nasty people intent on using our color against us, we are surrounded by perfectly nice people who embrace the color-blind ideal with a vengeance.

So what's to complain about? A steadily increasing stream of Black folk read these changes as proof that the old battles have been won and that we need a new politics that emphasizes individual initiative and a reduced role for government. If some of us haven't yet succeeded, the solution is to pull up our socks and try harder. Others, myself included, read the tea leaves rather differently. Yes, we have had our victories, but many of them have turned Pyrrhic. They have succeeded in making racism more subtle, so that disparities that once were clearly traceable to specific policies or heavy-handed practices now look much more like a series of individual failures. Therefore, what we need is a new political vision that continues to take race seriously even as we search for new ways to transform its significance.

Whatever our politics and however vulnerable we felt, we Black folk used to at least share the same geographic space. Bookies and accountants lived on the same block. Physicians and factory workers shopped in the same stores. Deacons and dishwashers utilized the same municipal services, paid for by the same tax base. We also had important institutions in common. We all went to the same churches. Our children went to the same schools. We hung out at the same Y. Although there were discernible differences in social class, aspirations often mattered more than money or position. Plumbers' daughters could be debutantes, and the president of the most "siditified" (translation: snootiest) Black social club in Denver was the custodian at my high school. We knew each other, talked to each other, and talked about each other when folk got out of line.

These days, the community is much less physically compact. Although most urban Black people continue to live in inner-city neighborhoods, increasingly folk who can afford to move out are opting to do so. By 1990, 32 percent of Blacks in metropolitan areas lived in the suburbs.[3] These migrants may return to the old neighborhood to get a haircut or visit family, but they go to the market, plant flowers, form social

networks, and raise their children elsewhere. In many parts of
the country, predominantly Black suburbs have sprung up.
While they provide a base for the furtherance of African-
American culture and opportunities for kinship and connect-
edness, they also redirect the interests and concerns of their
inhabitants. Instead of addressing the city's crumbling
schools, unsafe streets, and fiscal woes, the residents of places
like Cleveland Heights and Prince Georges County tend to
become focused on the issues facing their new "communities."[4]

Given these various changes, it is time for us to rethink
and reconsider the ties that bind. Perhaps we simply delude
ourselves when we continue to invoke the ideal of community.
My sense, however, is that if we make a mistake, it is in how
we conceive of community rather than in our continuing at-
tachment to it. We need to update our understanding of who
we are and where we are at. Like any family, the Black community has not remained static. Its contours have shifted. It
has a different location, metaphorical as well as physical. For
some people, the role the community plays in their lives has
changed significantly. This shouldn't surprise us. In any family, the way in which individual members connect to the
whole varies over time. But the fact that some folk move to
California and that others join a cult (or the Republican Party)
does not mean that the family ceases to exist or that the
prodigal members no longer belong.

Certainly, most of us continue to *feel* that we belong to
an overarching community. We experience *something,* so a useful starting point is to figure out what that something is. It
may be that in large part we are sensing our own need to
belong. If so, that is hardly cause for embarrassment. After all,

most human relationships are the result of internal as well as external forces, and it is often impossible to separate one from the other. We should also recognize that the answer may not be the same for everyone. For some, the essence of community may be our common culture. For others, our shared history may be key. For still others, a shared sense of oppression may continue to be important. The fact that the nature of the tie may vary from person to person or subgroup to subgroup does not mean that a powerful common bond cannot be forged. Even in the closest of families, different members connect to the whole in different ways.

In rethinking what we mean by community and what holds it together, we need to be honest about our differences. We can no longer act as if economic, social, cultural, and even national differences do not exist among us. We cannot treat as irrelevant the growth of a sizable Black middle class. We cannot simply mouth platitudes about the role of the Black church without paying attention to who is present on Sunday and who is not; without asking who is helped by the church on Monday and who is not. We who trace our lineage to slavery cannot continue to turn a deaf ear to immigrants from the Caribbean who insist that they are like us and not like us at the same time. We cannot ignore the vast differences in hope among our people.

We can no longer hide from the fact that there are Black folk whose politics are closer to Jesse Helms than Jesse Jackson. We need to admit that programs designed to help Black tenants may not necessarily help Black homeowners. We need to acknowledge that the day-to-day concerns of telephone company managers are not the same as those of people on welfare. We have to deal with the fact that for many young people today, the civil rights era is ancient history. For those who benefited from it, America looks like a land of milk and honey. For those whom the movement left behind, America is a war zone. We have to face up to the reality of "Black flight." It is critically important that we not define our community in such a way as to exclude those who have chosen to live apart from it physically but not emotionally. On the other hand, we must accept the fact that the nature of their tie will be different. Only then can we search for useful ways for our suburban kin to contribute to the life of the inner city.

We should also be honest about the fact that we are not all in the same boat when it comes to dealing with racial abuse. Some of us are shielded from it most of the time; others face it on a daily basis. Most of us live somewhere between those extremes. Even in situations where we do occupy the same boat, we differ greatly in our capacity to protect ourselves if and when it begins to take on water. Some of us are outfitted with life preservers, flares, and maybe even an inflatable raft, whereas others have no choice but to cling to the deck.

About half a dozen years ago, at a time when I still harbored the fantasy of becoming a playground legend, I severely dislocated a finger while guarding an out-of-control player as he drove to the basket. None of us had the nerve to try to yank it back in place (it looked pretty nasty) and the pain was eye-popping, so I immediately jumped in my car and went in search of medical assistance. I arrived at my HMO only to discover that the orthopedic group with which it had contracted had terminated its services a week earlier. Also, none of the people working in "urgent visit" felt competent to deal with my problem. So back in the car and over to the emergency room of a local hospital.

Like many emergency rooms in urban hospitals, this one was filled with a combination of trauma victims (a category in which I definitely placed myself) and poor families who use the emergency room as a source of primary care. Most of the people were Black or Latino. I watched TV and chitchatted with the people around me. Anything to keep my mind off the pain. After about forty-five minutes, my name was called. I spoke to the triage nurse and tried to sound as pitiful as possible, but the next thing I knew I was back in the large waiting room. Another hour passed. I thought about trying to pull rank and use my hospital connections to get seen before I passed out. But then I looked around me and realized that if I jumped the line, it just meant that other people in equally bad shape would have to wait that much longer. Also, I remembered that I didn't have any hospital connections anyway.

Two more hours passed. Finally my turn came. I was escorted into what seemed like a labyrinth of hallways and curtained-off areas. I was placed on a gurney, parked in a hallway, and told (erroneously) that someone would be with me shortly. For what seemed like forever, I watched Black and Brown people being wheeled back and forth, being talked down to when they were talked to at all, and in general being treated like slabs of meat. I tried to figure out how much of the palpable disrespect bordering on disdain was a reflection of emergency room culture in general and how much had to do with the vast racial and class gulf between the mostly White doctors and the mostly poor patients of color.

Eventually, I was wheeled in to see an orthopedist. He began asking me a series of perfunctory questions. Something about how I answered seemed to give him pause. He looked at me, really for the first time, and asked what I did for a living. Once he heard the L-word, his entire attitude changed. Instead of dealing with a basic Black man in a fonky T-shirt and basketball shoes, he was addressing a potential malpractice suit. Suddenly, he was Mister Affable. I had to hear about every lawyer he knew and every Yale professor he had ever met. He set a new world record in providing informed consent. It was almost enough to make me want to go back to being just another black slab of meat.

By paying attention to, rather than sliding over, our various differences, we are in a better position to reach out to all parts of the community. Instead of insisting that Carlton Banks (of *Fresh Prince* fame) quit the Dan Quayle fan club, leave Bel-Air behind, and in general learn to act more like his cousin Will, we should simply ask that he share his entrepreneurial talents and his checkbook with the community. If he is afraid to set foot in "the ghetto," we should tell him, "That's O.K., you can mail it in." Then, when the Carlton Banks Skills-Building Center is up and running in South Central Los Angeles, we can invite him there for the official grand opening (how could he resist?) and serenade him with a rap version of "For He's a Jolly Good Fellow."

In rethinking what defines our community and holds it together, we should not ignore the intangibles. Stephen Carter maintains that the tie that binds, the thing that draws very different people together, is a common love of our people.[5] That sounds right to me. It is not the whole story, but it is a critically important piece of it. A related wellspring of community is the sense of special obligation that most Black people feel toward one another.[6] I wish I could come up with a better word; "obligation" is so cold and formal, and sounds so, well, obligatory. But what I have in mind is the wonderful and scary and comforting and unnerving commitment that is at the heart of every worthwhile relationship. It is the promise to be there for one another; to honor one another; to "uplift" (to use an old-fashioned term) the race. I would add, as well, a third intangible. One definition of a feminist is "someone who believes women." In a similar vein, I think that the Black community consists of people who listen to, believe, and believe in one another, especially with respect to the impact of race in our lives. We listen critically when that is appropriate, and recognize blatant b.s. when we hear it, but our first instinct is not to discount, trivialize, or diminish. Nor do we assume that the victim's perspective is somehow more suspect than that of the perpetrator.

Of course, sentiments such as love and obligation can be perverted. Too often our unity has been reinforced by the notion that people should make certain sacrifices "for the sake of the race." In particular, Black folk who have grievances that might cast the community or an important part of it in a negative light are frequently asked to swallow them so as not to divert attention from the needs of the race as a whole. For example, gay men and lesbians have often been asked to put aside concerns about homophobia within the Black community. In effect, they are asked to give their racial identity priority over their sexual identity. But this assumes that the two are somehow separable. The impossibility of such a forced choice has been captured by the late Marlon Riggs in *Tongues*

Untied, a documentary by and about gay Black men. In the documentary, Riggs responds to a mythical, yet quite familiar, "race man" who wonders "[c]ome the final showdown, where does he face—Black or gay?" Riggs tells us: "You know the answer—the absurdity of that question. How can you sit in silence? How can you choose one eye over the other? This half of the brain over that? Or in words this brother might understand, which does he value most—his left nut or his right?"[7]

The fact that gay men and lesbians have, for the most part, tacitly accepted (or at least not challenged) the demand that they sacrifice in the name of solidarity does not mean that there is no harm done. A while back, Salt and Pepper was invited to sing at a tiny church in Connecticut's Naugatuck Valley. It was immediately apparent from the tambourine-to-parishioner ratio that people had come prepared to have church. And sure enough, the place rocked that evening. When it came time to bring the Word, a guest evangelist from out of state was introduced. She launched into a hellfire-and-brimstone sermon the likes of which I thankfully have not encountered before or since. Her basic message, delivered with extraordinary passion and skillful repetition, was that homosexuality is an abomination.

I considered standing up and saying something, but knew from good home training that that just isn't done in church, especially when you are a guest. So I glanced around at my fellow choir members, hoping through eye contact to at least establish a sense of shared discomfort. By and large, the Salts in the choir looked stunned. In contrast, the Peppers mostly looked blank, as if an invisible screen somehow kept the evangelist's words from penetrating. While I was trying to make sense of this, the strangest thing happened. A gay and indeed rather queenly young man who had accompanied one of the choir members on the trip suddenly became possessed of the spirit. He leaped up, threw back his hands, and started to shake. Then, with the rhythmic pattern of the hateful words forming an insistent back beat, he danced up and down the aisle, shouting praises to the Lord. The organist got into the act, and for several minutes he, the evangelist, and the young man played off one another until eventually the evangelist decided that it was time to wind down.

I have often thought back to that evening. I know full well that many of the Black folk in that church found the sermon repugnant and the young man's unconscious self-immolation painful to watch. Yet all of us managed to look as if it simply wasn't happening. My insides were leaping, but I probably displayed the same impassive gaze as everyone else. True, a church service is hardly an ideal time to enter into meaningful discussion, but even if the setting had been a Sunday-school class or a coffee-hour chat, most of us probably would have operated on the "this too shall pass" principle. That is because we recognize the extraordinary role—spiritual, political, and social—that the Black church plays in our collective lives. So we make sacrifices to keep it strong and unified. But the question is, at what cost? Who is asked to bear that cost? And are they any less the children of God than those folk whose needs the church more fully reflects?

Similarly, Black women have frequently been asked to sacrifice for the sake of the race. Contemporary examples abound. Alice Walker was pilloried in many quarters for her unflattering depictions of Black men in *The Color Purple*.[8] Whether there was truth behind the images was less important than that she dared to bring questions of gender subordination out into the open. Desiree Washington, the teenager whom boxer Mike Tyson was convicted of raping, was widely assailed for bringing down a Black man, and in particular for publicly reinforcing the image of Black men as sexually predatory.[9] Anita Hill was similarly taken to task. Her detractors included people who believed that she had testified truthfully and people who in any event questioned Clarence Thomas's fitness to serve.[10]

In each of these cases and countless more, anger at Black women who speak out is fueled by an acute awareness that Black men have been vilified throughout American history and are especially vulnerable today. Perhaps no phrase better captures the latter sentiment than the oft heard statement that "Black men are an endangered species." Therefore, runs the argument, we need to present Black men in the best light possible. At any rate, we certainly don't need to be tearing each other down and doing "the Man's" work for him. "These issues" should be dealt with "within the family."

I do not quarrel with the characterization of Black men as endangered. A couple of years ago Salt and Pepper was invited to participate in an anniversary concert honoring the young adult choir at a large New Haven church. It was one of those four-hour affairs where several guest choirs are invited to participate, and each sings three or four numbers that can stretch out for days if the Spirit is moving right. Anyway, as I cast my eyes around the sanctuary, I noticed two pews filled with young men in their twenties who looked simultaneously impassive and intent. They were serious. "How odd," I thought to myself, "you hardly ever see that many together-looking Black men of that age all in one place except in prison." Sure enough, when the men's choir was eventually introduced, it turned out that its members were indeed inmates at a nearby prison who had been furloughed in order to sing for this event.

A few months later, Salt and Pepper participated in a worship service at that very prison and shared the music ministry with that same choir. We then climbed into our cars, headed south, and after a brief stop at Micky D's, drove to Bridgeport, Connecticut, for an afternoon engagement. There we shared the program with another all-male singing group, the Bridgeport Boys Choir. They were already on their third number by the time we straggled in. The first thing I noticed was how young, innocent, and sweet they seemed. I then noticed how totally focused they were, notwithstanding their visible nervousness and apprehension. And they were good, musically speaking, very good. Suddenly and without warning, I found myself in tears. I tried to convince myself that they were tears of joy. After all, before me stood our community's future in the form of fifteen talented, ambitious, proud African-American males. But the truth is that I was awash in sadness, because the very same thing could be said about the young men I had worshipped with earlier in the day.

So I don't need to be convinced that Black men are an endangered species. But that is no reason to compel Black women to suffer in silence. Part of the reason that issues of gender domination have been played out in public is that we have never quite gotten around to addressing them in private. Furthermore, even if we believe that we should be presenting Black men in the best possible light, shouldn't we be presenting Black *women* in the best possible light as well? When presented with an image of womanhood that seemed to insist upon life on a pedestal, Sojourner Truth peeled it apart with a simple question: "Ain't I a woman?"[11] In similar fashion, women like Desiree Washington and Anita Hill might well ask, "Aren't we Black?" Like their male counterparts, Black women were brutalized during slavery. They too suffered in its aftermath. They too were lynched for being uppity.[12] They too have been consistently portrayed as being long on sexuality and short on morals. The "welfare queen" is just the latest version.[13] Although Black women may not be as endangered as Black men (especially if involvement in the criminal justice system is the measure), having to hold the fort in a war zone while the menfolk are absent is not exactly a picnic.

I realize that some of you are thinking, "If you care about Black women so much, why didn't you marry one?" That is a perfectly fair question, especially in light of my suggestion that love and obligation are wellsprings of community. The answer begins with the simple yet profound fact that I fell in love with a woman who is White. That, of course, doesn't end the matter, for I could have simply walked away, as other Black folk I know have done, out of a sense of obligation to the race. I, however, made a different choice. And I did so for the most selfish of reasons. With Jill, I felt confident that all of me would be welcome in the relationship: the part of me that is your basic Black man and the part that is not; the part that is outgoing and the part that is intensely private; the part that likes nice things and the part that abhors acquisitiveness; the part that cries at sad movies and the part that can be incredibly steely; the part that is playful and the part that takes life quite seriously. Jill is unique, and I knew

that I could learn a lot from her: about how to live out my
political commitments on a daily basis; about how to grow as
an individual at the same time; about how to be honest with
myself as well as with others; and about how to become more
spiritually open. Finally, I knew that our home would be a
refuge from the world, full of warmth and utterly lacking in
pretension. Could I have found this same mix of characteristics in a Black woman, one who was interested in me? Of
course. But whether I *would* have, and if so when, is far from
clear.

This still leaves two large questions unanswered. Notwithstanding everything I have just told you, did I marry Jill
at least in part *because* she is White? And in any event, should
I have put my own selfish interests aside for the sake of the
race? Not surprisingly, my answer to the first question is
"no," at least I don't think so. However, I know too much
about the human capacity for self-deception to pretend to
be any more certain than that. Without doubt, Jill's race
weighed in as a negative for me, if only because I don't exactly
enjoy having conversations like this one. That doesn't mean,
however, that it didn't weigh on the positive side as well, but
I don't think it did.

Some folks will never be convinced otherwise, of course.
Indeed Jill, of all people, may be among them. I was blown
away several months into our relationship when she asked me,
"Why are you dating a White woman?" "Do you mean why
am I dating you?" I answered lamely. "No, not me in particular. Why are you dating a White woman?" I don't remember
what I said, but I do remember that Jill didn't seem wholly
satisfied. And I have never thought to ask her whether her

doubts have since been allayed. But that conversation had a profoundly liberating effect on me, for it let me know that Jill saw and understood herself as a person with a race, and that she had no interest in trying to pretend that we could, or should, lead a color-blind or colorless existence.

As for the second question—whether I *should* have married Jill—I have exceedingly mixed feelings. If I were a rugged individualist, the answer would be easy. But I really do take seriously everything I said earlier about the importance of community, and of the Black community in particular. So my beliefs and my desires were very much in tension. Ultimately, I decided that if anything in life is personal, and therefore free from social obligation, it is our intimate relationships. And I took comfort in the fact that there are many, many ways to show love for my people. Nevertheless, I was, and remain, acutely aware that, in symbolic terms, marrying outside the race is easily seen as a rejection of Black people, and of Black women in particular. And symbols matter.

On occasion, the fact that I am married to Jill has caused people to shut down, and to tune out what I have to say. I remember especially vividly a talk I gave on the nature of the AIDS epidemic in communities of color. As quite often happens when I speak to health-care providers, my comments seemed to split the audience. Most of the White listeners looked uncomfortable and mildly stunned as I talked about racism, paternalism, exploitation, and mistrust. On the other hand, the Blacks and Latinos in the room practically cheered me on. With one exception. I noticed that halfway through my remarks, one Black woman, who had been hanging on to my every word, seemed to jump ship. Later, during a break in the conference I overheard a conversation between that same woman and another sister who had been singing my praises. "But he said he's married to a White woman!" said the ship jumper. "I didn't hear that," responded her companion. "Yes, he said it." "So what. I thought he was great." "But he's married to a White woman." Quite obviously, she couldn't care less whether I had anything useful to say. As far as she was concerned, my stuff was counterfeit.

As it happens, I had not said that I was married to a White woman, or that I was married at all (although I was wearing a wedding band). Instead, I had observed in passing that I live in a mixed neighborhood, that most of my colleagues are White, and that I live in a largely integrated world. "Why, I even play basketball with White guys," I had said puckishly. My point, which I eventually made explicit, was that I shouldn't be dismissed as a fringy separatist. I had quite consciously not mentioned my marriage to Jill, who was present at the conference in her own right, so as to avoid producing the very reaction that got stirred anyway. So much for attempting to control audiences.

In rethinking what we mean by "the community," we should be as inclusive as possible. We should resist the temptation to draw lines based on categorical assumptions about who is or is not for real, and to subordinate the interests and concerns of any subgroup. After all, none of us has a superior claim on the race. Besides, if we cannot deal with difference within the family, how can we expect White folk to deal with us?

We should be ever mindful that the very act of defining a community also defines who stands outside it. It is perfectly

appropriate to conceive of the community in a way that excludes Black folk who choose not to "identify" with the race.
They might still be Black, thanks to their ancestry and phenotype, but that fact does not necessarily mean that they should
be regarded as members of the Black "community." By definition, such folk shouldn't get too choked up over their exclusion. Indeed, when people who don't identify nevertheless
complain about not being included, they can usually be dismissed as provocateurs. On the other hand, when we excom-
municate people who truly long to belong, we often wind up
poisoning our own well. Some of the most vitriolic critics of
programs broadly supported within the community are Black
folk who have been made to feel less than fully welcome by
their own kind.

Even in drawing the line between those who wish to
belong and those who do not, we should be careful not to
judge too quickly or too harshly. Remember the first-year law
student who took umbrage at the assumption that she wished
to be part of the Black students' organization? As it turns out,
she showed up in my classroom later that day. I don't know
whether she would have self-selected herself into my company, but she had no choice. The course was required and
students were assigned to classes according to some formula
known only to the registrar.

From day one, I had a hunch "Pam" might be the one I
had heard so much about. There was something proudly independent about her, and she seemed almost willfully indifferent to me. Over time, I discovered that she was delightfully
contrary, quite apart from race, and that she had an abhor-
rence of pigeonholes of whatever type. Pam quickly let me

know that many of her political views were probably much more conservative than mine, and I allowed as how her revelation did not come as much of a shock. Once we got that out of the way, the shield came down and we interacted comfortably and easily.

Near the end of the term, the class discussion veered off into a discussion of race. I think the conversation got started during a mid-class break, and then kept going even after everyone returned to the room. Sensing that few of the students were all that eager to get back to civil procedure, and aware that everyone seemed engaged, I let the discussion run its course. As I was making some point or other, I mentioned in passing that I had nodded to another Black person on the street. "Do you mean to say," asked one of the White students, "that you speak to people on the street just because they are Black?" I had never quite thought of it that way, but I said, "Yes, I guess I do." Then one of the Black students said, "I do too." And a second Black student said, "Me too, especially when I am someplace I haven't been before, or when I am in a neighborhood where Blacks are in the minority."

He had scarcely finished speaking when the word "Oh!" filled the room. That one syllable lasted for nearly five seconds and began to descend in pitch halfway through. It was the unmistakable sound of recognition. I turned around to behold Pam, her eyes dancing and her face the picture of wonderment. "So that's what it means," she said to no one in particular. "All this time people kept speaking to me and I just assumed they thought they knew me and were just mistaken. Oh!"

I marveled at how clearly delighted Pam was to learn

this little bit of Black culture, much more so than were the White students. And then it hit me. "Oh!" I exclaimed to myself. "That's it!" All this time I had assumed that because Pam looks and is Black, she knew how to "be" Black. I'm not talking about being able to "throw down" or anything like that. I mean basic stuff, like noticing one another, acknowledging one another, and various other forms of kinship ritual. I had assumed that she had rejected all that was typically Black. It never occurred to me that she was largely ignorant of it. Later I learned that Pam's Black Trinidadian father played no role in her upbringing. She was raised by her White mother in an all-White neighborhood.

All of a sudden her opening-day gaffe took on a new light. On one level, she didn't fully comprehend how insulting it would be to other Black students to have their proffer of kinship rejected. At another level, Pam was right in questioning what assumptions the other Black students had made about her. Did they really know anything about her, and would they like what they found out? She was also right in wondering whether she would feel comfortable in BALSA, although a smoother approach would have been to simply thank the second-year student for her concern and then play things by ear. In part, Pam was probably just being contrary, but I suspect that in even larger part she was asking a straightforward question in an attempt to learn how other Black people think about race. So, when all is said and done, I think it would have been a mistake to write Pam off in spite of her seeming desire to set herself apart. The broader lesson is that we should err on the side of inclusion whenever there is any doubt.

TAKE STOCK
OF OUR CULTURE

A couple of years ago, while channel surfing I happened upon *ComicView,* a showcase for stand-up comics on cable's Black Entertainment Television (BET). I put down the remote and watched host D. L. Hughley do his thing. After messing with the studio audience and doing a bit or two, he announced the next guest artist, whose stage name is Just June. She was a good-looking fortyish woman with great bone structure and a sophisticated short natural. You could easily imagine her heading up a division of a medium-sized company. Except for the impish grin on her face. And the dancing eyes. But once June began her routine, it was obvious that she was right where she belonged. She was kickin' it; without doubt a down-home girl working a down-home crowd. She had a sneaky sense of humor, and her timing was extraordinary. One moment you'd be wondering where she was headed, and the next you'd be falling out of the chair.

June ended her routine by recalling how just the other day while she was out driving, a White man in a convertible had yelled out to her at a stoplight, "Hey, nigger." She described how her blood began to rise and she started to plot her revenge when all of a sudden it struck her: "Hey, maybe he was just trying to relate to me." At that point the audience looked dumbfounded. June waited an extra beat or two, then explained, "After all, with all these Black folk coming on national TV and saying nigger this and nigger that, how's he supposed to know that's not what we *want* to be called." The studio erupted in laughter. Then, as the audience calmed down, she delivered the capper. "I really don't think that Martin and Malcolm died so that we could go around calling each other nigger on television." After a brief pause to take it all in, the audience burst into sustained applause.

Later in the same show, as D. L. Hughley engaged in patter before introducing another comic, he quite casually used the N-word several times, to the audience's seeming delight. I shouldn't have been surprised, since that is an integral part of his style. When he is doing stand-up, Hughley (who eventually left the show and landed a major sitcom role) regularly uses "nigger"—once per minute or more when he gets going[1]—in the same way that others might use "guy." For example, when teasing a man about how he is dressed, he would say, "That nigger know he clean!" Or when trying to describe brutally hot weather he would say something like "Niggers be passing out everywhere." His brand of humor reflects his street roots[2] and creates a bond of intimacy with much of the audience, as if we all were just hanging out on the corner together. But, as June so craftily pointed out, that street corner is being telecast nationally to millions of people, many of whom look just like the guy at the stoplight.

The Black community is at a cultural crossroads. Like the *ComicView* audience, we are confused, and not just about the N-word. Part of the problem is that our culture is no longer ours alone. Of course, it never was exclusively ours. Although African in origin, African-American culture has been mostly made in America. And like all subcultures but especially those that are homegrown, it exists in a complicated relationship to the dominant culture. Nevertheless, despite the fact that we have always been linked, today more than ever we are locked in a complicated tango with the cultural mainstream.

For much of our history, African-American culture benefited from its invisibility to White America. So long as our customs, rituals, social practices, and modes of expression did not pose problems for the larger society, we were usually left alone to develop and enjoy them in relative obscurity. Every once in a while the White cognoscenti developed an interest in us—the Harlem Renaissance stands out in this regard—and there were undoubtedly particular art forms, jazz for one, that were carried along by White support. But for the most part distance, separation, and basic disinterest were cultural facts of life. At the same time, proximity, a deep sense of connection, and the absence of available alternatives meant that Black folk of every stripe were rooted in, and contributed to, their own culture.

With the growth of mass media, however, especially television, Black folk have lost the shelter of the shadows. What we do and say gets noticed these days, including what we say about each other and how we talk to one another. It took a while. When I was in high school, you could watch television all day long without seeing a Black face. When the sponsors finally decided that Ipana toothpaste sales wouldn't plummet if a person of color (other than Ricky Ricardo) graced the screen, the first roles were hardly windows onto Black America. But *Julia* and *I Spy* have given way to *Roc* and *Living Single;* the occasional appearance of a Sam Cooke or Godfrey Cambridge on the *Ed Sullivan Show* has been replaced by *Video Soul* and *Def Comedy Jam.* And *Jet* magazine, which you used to have to purchase at the corner store, is now on-line and can be accessed via Lexis/Nexis.

All this wouldn't matter if no one but Black folk were paying attention. But contemporaneous White interest in the Harlem Renaissance pales in comparison to White interest in today's African-American art forms. If White folk ceased to flock to his movies, I'm not sure that New York Knicks superfan Spike Lee could still afford front-row seats at Madison Square Garden. Similarly, the investment portfolios of Tupac Shakur, Dr. Dre, and Snoop Doggy Dogg would be substantially reduced if their music stayed within the family, given that half or more of rap albums are sold to young White males,[3] just as the majority of viewers of *Def Comedy Jam* are White.[4] More surprisingly still, across the country in places like Morocco, Indiana, and Bridgetown, Ohio, White teenagers who call themselves (or are labeled) "wiggers" are embracing not only rap music but also hip-hop modes of dress, speech, and self-presentation.[5]

Even as White people are checking out African-American culture and absorbing (if not appropriating) large portions of it, we seem bent on embracing the worst aspects of America's mass culture. Too many of us have bought into the notion that if we just had the right shoes or the right jacket or the right car, we would rule the world. We have replaced the

God of Abraham, Jacob, Sarah, and Rachel with the gods of
consumption and acquisition and self-centeredness. We worship the golden calf. At the same time, we have lost touch
with the values and rhythms that sustained us through both
slavery in fact and slavery by another name.

In many ways, we have become the quintessential Americans, except that the urge to consume and acquire is supposed
to be offset by a faith in the future that leads to sacrifice and
delayed gratification. Unfortunately, for many of us such faith
would be absurd, given present circumstances. The result is
that a large chunk of our community is powerless, disaffected,
acquisitive without the means to acquire, and culturally untethered. We may be a little ahead of the curve, but if America does not restructure her economy and enter into a period of
cultural and spiritual rebirth, we just may be the wave of the
future. Certainly lots of working-class White folk are not far
behind us on the road to alienation.[6]

One consequence of our being on display at the very
moment that we have begun to lose our moorings is that our
culture has come in for a barrage of criticism leveled by folk
who don't necessarily have our best interests at heart. The
indictment is long. We don't value hard work; we prefer being on welfare to working; we expect something for nothing;
we have babies just so that we can get government support;
we scoff at marriage; we are indifferent to the prospect of
babies having babies; violence is our way of life; we are sexist,
homophobic, and anti-semitic. The take-home message is
clear: most of our problems are of our own making. At a
minimum, we are not doing our part to resolve them. And in
any event, we are not as noble as we pretend to be.

The enthusiasm with which this critique has been embraced by a broad spectrum of White America is truly scary. I can't help but believe that White folk find it attractive primarily because it points the finger at us and away from them. If we are busily destroying ourselves, we can no longer claim the moral high ground that characterized the civil rights movement. If we are not doing our part to solve our own problems, then how can we expect White America to make sacrifices on our behalf? If we are guilty of bias toward others, including some of our own, then what better justification could there be for sitting on the sidelines and, well, gloating just a little?

Our cultural disarray is exacerbated by our lack of cohesion. The fragmentation of our community has made it difficult for us to enter into robust internal debate about cultural matters without the discussion prematurely being taken public in ways that hurt us. It also has lessened our capacity to support community-based cultural institutions. It has weakened our ability to transmit our culture by word of mouth. And it has resulted in the transplantation of many African-Americans far from their cultural roots.

Finally, we are experiencing a profound disconnect between the generations. At issue is more than the traditional insistence by parents that their children "turn that awful music down." The rupture has less to do with taste in music, clothes, language, or manners than it does with the messages our young people are conveying. Beyond your basic youthful confusion, rebellion, and swagger, their cultural output tells a story of hopelessness, lifelessness, aimlessness, and despair. It tells us straight out that our children do not have a future, or at least none we would wish for them or for ourselves. It tells us that their present is painful and hard. The beltless-baggy-pants prison look would be merely hip (or weird, depending on your taste) if it weren't for the fact that many of our young children develop their fashion sense firsthand on visiting day at the county jail. Too many of them will eventually slide all too easily from visitor to visited. Many of us old fogeys don't want to hear this. It clashes with the vision of progress that has sustained us for so long. It suggests that our struggles have made little difference whatsoever in the lives of young folk who could be, or who are, our sons and daughters.

For all these reasons and more, we desperately need to take stock of our culture. It is already the subject of much debate. We would be foolish not to weigh in. On a more affirmative note, as the prime beneficiaries of African-American culture, we have a powerful interest in the shape it assumes. We should make sure that our culture matches who we are and what we need at this point in our collective evolution. Finally, if we are indeed serious about getting rid of racial hierarchy, we need to have a better handle on which parts of our culture we want to preserve in more or less their present form and which parts we are willing to toss into the American stew. Fear of cultural loss is one of the hidden reasons that many of us are apprehensive about making peace with White America. If we cease to be defined as an "other," will we lose our cultural distinctiveness as well?

With respect to our generation gap, we need to take it more seriously and to approach it in all its complexity. We have made an impressive start in the debate that has grown up around Gangsta Rap. Hundreds of Black ministers around the country, the most visible of whom is Rev. Calvin O. Butts III of Harlem's Abyssinian Baptist Church, have organized protests against albums that glory in violence and debase women.[7] They have been joined by various mainstream Black political organizations, as well as by Black radio stations that target a broad cross section of the Black community.[8]

To their credit, many of the ministers, and less surprisingly the radio executives, have taken care to emphasize that rap music in general is not the target. Rev. Frederick D. Haynes III, pastor of Friendship West Baptist Church in Oak Cliff, Texas, makes it plain. "I am not against the idiom of rap music. As a matter of fact, I think it's a powerful means of cultural expression that continues our oral tradition, which is part of our history as black people. But I am adamantly opposed to the toxic content that comes from rap groups such as the Geto Boys and others that disrespect and dis our African-American sisters by treating them as pieces of meat."[9] Nor have the critics of Gangsta Rap let the music industry executives off the hook, "the big wheels," according to Rev. Haynes, "who sit up in the corporate offices of these major recording companies and who not only allow this but who promote this and are willing to pay our young African-American brothers and sisters to contribute to the lynching of the minds of our people."[10] Nevertheless, responds Rev. Sheron C. Patterson, pastor of Oak Cliff's Crest-Moore King United Methodist Church, "[w]e have to be responsible for ourselves. This is black men calling black women ho's and bitches— ain't nobody white involved."[11]

The debate has not been one-sided. Rap artists and culture critics have vigorously defended Gangsta Rap as an unvarnished depiction of life on the street.[12] My own sense of the matter is that the ministers easily have the better of the argument insofar as unredeemably misogynist lyrics are concerned, and may well be right regarding violence, although the "we're just telling it like it is" defense has some force. On the other hand, Gangsta Rap's critics are on much weaker ground when it comes to challenging lyrics that are "vulgar" or are "contrary to the progress and goals of African-Americans."[13] But more important than a scorecard is the fact that a dialogue has begun. At its best, it has ignored the temptation to dwell on what White Americans might be making of all this, and has focused instead on what the Gangsta genre reveals about the slice of the community it seeks to depict. The utter disrespect for women comes through loud and clear, but so too does the rappers' fragile sense of self-respect. Also evident is the narrowness of the rappers' sense of community, and the failure of the critics to welcome them into a wider world.

We should treat the flap over Gangsta Rap as a target of opportunity. It is a chance to bridge the generation gap and search for a common place to stand. A hopeful starting point is a joint exploration of the role of artists in building community. We should follow the lead of folk like Representative Maxine Waters and Rev. Benjamin Chavis, who for some time have been urging their peers to sit down with disaffected young people and ask them how they see the world and what they might do to improve upon it. We fogeys should encourage them to speak to our concerns by demonstrating that we care about theirs. We should admit the ways in which we have failed them, and encourage them to do better by the even younger youth who look up to them. We should pass the torch, and urge them to be more responsible by handing responsibility to them.

In thinking through the implications for our culture of the Black community's increasing fragmentation, it is important to remember that culture itself is one of the ties that bind. Just as social splintering weakens our cultural base, cultural dissolution weakens our sense of community. Therefore, just as we need to shore up our community for the sake of our culture, we need to shore up our culture for the sake of our community.

It is not uncommon these days for African-Americans to rely on mass media, especially the tube, to sustain us culturally. The more disconnected we are from the physical community, the more we rely on Martin Lawrence to teach us the latest slang, on Donnie Simpson and Bill Bellamy to keep us connected musically, and on the Black media to keep us generally informed. The resultant centralization may well be advantageous in creating a common cultural core, but it may also rob the culture of some of its improvisational quality. And of course relying on mass media for the transmission of a subculture raises the kinds of knotty problems voiced by June on *ComicView*. We aren't the only ones watching. One of our challenges is to sort out the risks and opportunities of taking the culture public.

When our culture comes under attack, we need to respond both to our accusers and to the problems they highlight. We should use the occasion to point out efforts that have long been underway in our community to deal with the highlighted problem. Teen pregnancy is an excellent example. Often we will need to set the record straight, as when the dimensions of our reliance on welfare are grossly exaggerated, or it is seriously suggested that Black women (or any women, for that matter) have additional children in order to collect the modest increment in AFDC. But sometimes we should treat the criticisms as a wake-up call, even if they are false in part and intended to disparage.

That is no easy matter. Virtually all Black people would like to shed what we regard as cultural pathologies, if only we could do so without providing fuel to our enemies. But what is a pathology and what is a sensible adaptation? What is ours and what is the dominant culture's? For example, is it fair to accuse Black women (or any women) of becoming "dependent" on welfare if there are no jobs to be had, or if remaining on welfare is the only way for a mother to ensure that her children have access to health care? And even when we do acknowledge that something is part of our culture, that does not end the inquiry. As Margareth Etienne has so trenchantly put it: "We need to distinguish between those things that are worth keeping and those that are merely a bad habit."

In sorting out how to deal with the pull of mass culture, we probably have to accept that we alone cannot hush its siren song. But we can build up our own cultural counterforce to it. Where possible, we should shore up those traditional values, customs, and institutions that have carried us across the river Jordan so many times. We should also not hesitate to create new customs, like Kwanzaa, that give old values new life. I have been amazed at how quickly Kwanzaa has caught on and how broadly it is practiced by friends from across the African-American spectrum, however measured. Clearly we hunger for rituals that bring us together and that remind us of the importance of communal effort and collective responsibility. What could be more wonderfully un-American?

Finally, we need to think through the implications of trying to carry out this cultural reexamination in plain view of millions of spectators and a provocateur or two. We have to get on with it, but are there any precautions we should take or rules of the road we should follow? I can think of three, and would welcome suggestions for more. First, we should resist false appeals to balance. We may well come across issues with respect to which we are evenly divided or are evenly split along multiple lines. In such instances, a full airing of every point of view is of course appropriate. With respect to other issues, however, there may be relatively little division. Ninety percent of the community may line up on one side, five percent on the other, with the remaining five indifferent. If so, the dissenting five percent deserve a hearing, and indeed may have the better of the argument, but it would be a mistake to claim that they should be given equal time. I can't tell you how many times I have tuned in to the *MacNeil-Lehrer NewsHour* when there was a panel discussing some issue of special relevance to the Black community and discovered that in order to achieve "balance" half the panel is stacked with folk whose views are marginal at best.

My second caution regarding the public assessment of our culture is that we should resist the temptation to simplify our views to make them more readily digestible or to hide their difficulties. Too often the bright lights lead perfectly intelligent people to substitute pap for thought, or to round off so many edges that whatever they had to say of value just rolls away. My final caution is the mirror opposite. We should resist the temptation to make issues more complex than they need to be. Again, the bright lights sometimes lead us to pile refinement onto refinement until the basic point sinks under the weight. In my office hangs one of my favorite posters. Along the bottom are the words "How to improve a duck." Above them stands your basic duck outfitted in a jaunty yellow rain hat and duck boots. He looks perfectly happy, but somehow I doubt it.

Once we are confident that our culture is strong and vibrant and serves us well, we can interact with the mainstream culture without fear of being swallowed up or taken over by it. We can also then take advantage of aspects of mainstream culture without guilt. Lots of us already do plenty of "white" things, but we worry that somehow they detract from our African-American heritage, or perhaps just our image. The more secure we are about that heritage, and the more it reflects where our community is today, the farther we can range without fear of becoming untethered.

In the summer of 1989 a hardy band of Black, Latino, and Asian-American law professors gathered for four days at a retreat center in Wisconsin. We had the somewhat audacious goal of reenvisioning how law should approach race in the post-civil rights era. The fruits of that labor have since come to be known as Critical Race Theory. The gathering was marked by much rhetoric tossing and idea mongering as befits a summer camp for academics, but we also did a lot of bonding, mostly in the form of informal group sings.

Each night, we would gather in a conference room or a hallway or under the stars and harmonize. Mostly we sang spirituals and 1960s rhythm and blues. By the third day we had pretty much exhausted our collective repertoire but not our desire for each other's company. Then, out of the blue, someone suggested that we sing a show tune. I forget which one. "Who let in the geek?" I thought. But since I happened to know the song, I joined in so as to save the person from humiliation. As it turned out, everyone knew the song. At first I sang it tentatively, partly to give the impression that I didn't know it well, and partly because I was still trying to figure out whether we should be singing this "white bread" song. Others seemed tentative as well, probably for similar reasons. But as we worked our way toward the refrain we began singing with the gusto befitting show music, and by the time we finished Ethel Merman would have been proud. That one song led to another and another, and before we knew it we had stayed up much too late for people of our advanced age. And in spite of our spirited foray into the heart of Americana, we awoke in the morning still able to pursue our critical mission.

WELCOME THE NEW
KIDS ON THE BLOCK

It is high time we began a frank and open dialogue with the folks with whom we share the bottom of the hill. For too long we have viewed other people of color primarily as rivals for "the crumbs that fall from the master's table." Occasionally, we have sought to unite with them around common interests as we define them, but it doesn't take much for us to lapse back into a thinly disguised free-for-all. At best, we tend to ignore the rest of the rainbow, despite the efforts of Jesse Jackson and a few others to build bridges. It is remarkable how little we know about other people of color. We, and they, have been so fixated on our relationships with White America that we have failed to engage each other.

But there is more to the story than just externally forged rivalry and massive disengagement. Many Black folk are sincerely of the view that we *deserve* more from society than do other people of color. First off, we are entitled to special treatment because we are America's largest racial minority. Needless to say, this claim is a bit inconvenient in places like

Miami and Los Angeles, and will be untrue across the board in forty years or so. More fundamentally, the logic of the claim is far from self-evident. In fact, a pretty decent argument can be made that the larger a group is, the less protection it needs from majority tyranny. Then there is the view that we are entitled to special consideration because we have been standing in line longer than anyone else. If you don't count Native Americans. On the other hand, we may have gained certain advantages by being here first, not least of which is that we have had plenty of time to figure out how to work the system.

One of our favorite trumps is that, unlike other people of color, we were brought to America's shores involuntarily. The implication is that the horrors of the middle passage and the unseemliness of our having been kidnapped or purchased entitle us to a special measure of solicitude and respect. (Once again, we conveniently leave out Native Americans, who hopelessly complicate the picture.) However, the difficulty with relying on our forced importation is that no African-American living today came by slave ship, and neither did any of our parents. Nor is it exactly the case that most Latinos and Asian-Americans arrived on the *QE 2*. To take just one contemporary example, several times in recent years vessels teeming with Chinese asylum seekers have made it to our shores. The circumstances of their passage have proved horrific, and we have learned to our dismay that these would-be Americans often were indentured to the people who arranged for their escape. True, the United States government was not implicated in their exploitation (by, for example, facilitating trafficking in human beings), but that fact did not make the new arrivals' voyage any more pleasant.

We also invoke the experience of slavery and its grim aftermath as a basis for favoring us over other people of color. We have suffered the greatest deprivation, historically, and therefore deserve the most in reparations. That may well be a legitimate argument, assuming there are reparations to be had. But the truth is that most of us are not in any position to draw meaningful comparisons. We are largely ignorant of the history of other people of color. Most Black people know very little, for example, about coolie labor laws, about the slavery-like conditions of many migrant labor camps, or about the Trail of Tears, the forced relocation of the Cherokee Nation during which a fourth of the population died.[1]

Nor do we fare much better when we glibly assert that in contemporary America, Blacks are worse off than other people of color. Most of us know very little about Laotian, Bangladeshi, or other Asian-American communities that are visibly struggling to survive. And even though we do know that many Latinos and Native Americans are having a hard time of it, we conveniently forget that fact when we are trying to stay at the front of the parade of color. Finally, we aren't above playing the nativist card. We deserve to be elevated above Asian-Americans and Latinos because we are more truly American than they. After all, English is our native tongue. We go back several generations. Although our distant African heritage is important to us, we owe no allegiance to any other country. Of course, in trading on the fact that many Whites view Asian-Americans and Latinos as foreign even if they are American-born,[2] we implicitly recognize that at least in that respect they are worse off than we are.

Quite apart from our sense that we are more deserving

than other people of color, Black people tend to resent what we often perceive as the unfair advantages possessed by other people of color. In particular, many Blacks believe that Latinos are more "acceptable" to White society by virtue of their lighter color (on average). I am reminded of a ditty I often heard as a child. "If you are white, you're all right. If you're brown, stick around. If you're black, stay back." Although this bit of wisdom was usually offered as a commentary on color consciousness *within* the Black community, it captures our sense of external color consciousness as well. Many of us also begrudge Asian-Americans their relative success in commerce and in the classroom. We discount their effort and determination and cast about for less attractive explanations. Even if we do not resent them directly, we take justifiable umbrage at the fact that the accomplishments of Asian-Americans are constantly flung in our faces by White folk bent on mischief. More generally, we are not happy at the prospect of being leapfrogged by groups we thought were beneath us or at best beside us in the pecking order. And we truly get perturbed when we sense that the new kids on the block disdain or disrespect us.

Our resentment frequently expresses itself in a lack of charity. Too often we speak of Korean-American and Asian-Indian merchants in the same unflattering terms we employed to describe Jewish shopkeepers thirty years ago. Many of our stand-up comics seem to think that burlesquing an Asian accent is a clever thing to do, and too often their audiences reward them with laughter. We take perverse pleasure in the fact that many Latinos have to struggle at least as much as we do. We give Native Americans a break, partly because we are more aware of their oppression, but in large part because we do not ordinarily consider them a threat to us.

It is critically important for Black folk to own up to these sentiments and to question our assumptions and beliefs about other communities of color. It is also important for Latinos, Asian-Americans, and Native Americans to engage us around these issues and to put their own stuff on the table as well. If we do not explore the real differences that exist among us, we will never discover what we truly have in common. We cannot in good conscience insist that White folk take up the cause of racial justice if we are not equally willing to struggle with the issues of pecking order and bias among ourselves. And as we head into a century in which we collectively will become the majority, we need to make sure that we develop new patterns of relating so that we do become enmeshed in an even more complex version of king of the hill.

PART FIVE

The Promised Land

Suppose we had a magic wand with which we could instantaneously change America's racial landscape. How would we use it? Would we eliminate race altogether? All at once, or over time? Would we retain race, but alter its meaning, and if so, in what way? Would we alter people's life circumstances (by, for example, eliminating disparities in income) in order to eliminate the continuing effects of our old conceptions of race?

If we were to create a racial Promised Land, what would it look like? What would it feel like? What would it be like? Who would inhabit America's great cities? Who would inhabit her suburbs and her countryside? What would families look like? High schools? University physics departments? What would the typical workplace look like? Who would be the bosses and who the underlings? Who would be the NBA's post-up players and the NHL's goalies? What would be the makeup of the three largest churches in town? The three smallest? The three nearest synagogues? The U.S. Senate? The

New York Philharmonic orchestra? The top groups on *Video Soul?*

If you are like me, these questions are not all that easy to answer. We human beings tend to become quite attached to the familiar, with all of its warts and blemishes. At least we know how to negotiate it. We know what to expect. We have already figured out how to adapt to the bad and take advantage of the good. Even the negatives often have a positive face. For example, while it is regrettable that for many Black youth athletic prowess seems to be their only ticket out of poverty and away from the pressures of the street, one consequence of this truncated set of choices is that Black athletes have come to dominate in several professional sports. Sure, it might be great to have more Black physics teachers, but there is something wonderful (as in full of wonder) about the physics-defying artistry of a Charles Barkley or an Anfernee Hardaway.

Then there is a second difficulty. If we fiddle with race, what are the implications for ethnicity, and in particular for ethnic culture? For African-Americans, separating race and ethnicity is difficult to do, largely because so much of our culture arose out of our struggle to survive in the face of racial domination. If racism were no longer a fact of life, how would our culture be affected? Would, for example, the blues be the same? If instead of living primarily in areas of heavy Black concentration we were scattered evenly across every neighborhood in America, would African-American culture suffer?

The implications for White ethnics are also far from clear. In many ways, race has served to dampen inter-ethnic antagonisms and to moderate populist impulses. Historically, when White hyphenated-Americans have experienced economic hardship, they have been encouraged to vent their frustrations on people of color rather than on each other or, worse, on Whites who are doing well. Therefore, if racial scapegoating were somehow eliminated, it is conceivable that Whites might divide along lines marked by group identity or economic self-interest. Similarly, if Asian-Americans and Latinos no longer had to be concerned with a race-based pecking order, long-standing ethnic antagonisms (e.g., Chinese versus Japanese) and newer ethnic rivalries (e.g., Puerto Ricans versus Chicanos) might well become more pronounced.

Finally, it is hard to figure out what exactly would have to change in order to truly eliminate racism and transform the meaning of race. Consider the following thought experiment. Imagine that there exists a planet called Beigia which is an exact replica of Earth. Everything about the two planets is identical, from their celestial origins to their location in the solar system, from the composition of their atmosphere to the last blade of grass. The planets are indistinguishable in every way imaginable. Every country on Earth has a Beigian counterpart. So does every village and every hamlet. Names, places, and events are exactly the same. When a dog barks here, a dog barks there. Each of us Earthlings has an exact counterpart on Beigia, someone who looks, thinks, acts, feels, and lives just like us.

One day, a strange thing happens in Beigia. Instantaneously and without warning, everyone turns an identical shade of—you guessed it—beige. What is more, everyone's hair, facial features, and body type are instantly transformed so as to eliminate all racial differences. It is as if someone mixed three parts Mariah Carey to one part Connie Chung. Mind you, everyone continues to have individually distinctive features and to be readily recognizable to all who knew them before. And family members continue to resemble one another. But the physical differences that distinguish one person from another or that mark a family as related no longer fall into racial patterns. Similarly, accents, dialects, and speech patterns are altered in ways that blur race while leaving class, region, and general fluency as detectable as before.

Has race ceased to exist on Beigia? Has its meaning changed? Probably not. On a practical level, so long as people remember who used to be what, or have ready access to such information, race can continue to be a potent social force. To be sure, sorting by race would become much more cumbersome. Moreover, in the absence of an apartheid-style identity card system, keeping track would become increasingly more difficult over time as memories faded and people moved from place to place. Given the absence of visual cues, intermarriage would be harder to detect as well.

On the other hand, if individuals wished to be identified with a race, they could easily do so by, for example, dressing in particular colors the way street gangs do. People also could indirectly reveal their race by adhering to ethnic patterns. For example, it wouldn't take a genius to figure out that folk who celebrate the feast day of St. Stanislaus are probably Polish and therefore White, or that folk who celebrate Cinco de Mayo are probably Latino. But then there would be little to stop people from "passing," by wearing the colors of a different race or mimicking a different ethnicity, so long as no one who "knew them when" ratted on them.

How much different would life be on the planet Beigia? For one thing, racial identity would be considerably more fluid. Individuals would have a great deal more choice in the matter than they do on the planet Earth. Also, racial discrimination would become increasingly less common, as race became harder to detect. As far as ethnicity is concerned, Whites would be free to embrace it if they wished, since they would suffer few adverse effects from "outing" themselves racially. People of color, however, would face something of a Hobson's choice: they could gain the benefits of racial invisibility only by forgoing race-revealing aspects of their ethnic culture.

Let's take another step. Suppose that along with the physical changes, Beigians lose all memory related to racial identity. Quite simply, they no longer remember who used to be what and can no longer make the connection between ethnicity and race. Imagine, as well, that all references in public and private records to an individual's race have been magically deleted or changed to "human." With these refinements, has the meaning of race been transformed on Beigia? The answer, I think, is "yes, no, and yes." "Yes" in the literal sense that there is no memory of race and no way to track it. "No" in the sense that the existing crop of Beigians would already have been marked by race. Each Beigian would unwittingly carry her historical race forward into the raceless future to the extent that it affects where she is positioned in society, how prepared she is to meet life's challenges, and how she sees and interprets the world around her. "Yes" in that although past racial advantages and disadvantages would persist, the social pecking order would no longer be based on race. Thus (former) people of color who managed to succeed at the game of "catch up" would not have to worry about racism asserting itself again.

Would we want to live on Beigia? Racial discrimination would be a thing of the past. Equal opportunity would be abundant, although some folks would have a considerable head start. Given the fact that race is untraceable, no one could be blamed for the racial ills of the past. Nor would anyone be in a position to point the finger. People who started out behind the pack might well wonder whether their poor position was the result of past racial inequity, but there would be no way to demonstrate it.

All in all, Beigia sounds like an extraordinary place. No racism. No bigotry. Not even any racial tension. What could be better? Nevertheless, I'd be willing to bet the ranch that most of us, myself included, would have very little interest in trading places with our Beigian counterparts and would much prefer to stay right here on good old deficient Earth.

Why is that? I'm not exactly sure. In part our resistance reflects the artificiality of the thought experiment itself. And in part it reflects the sheer massiveness of the changes we would have to make and the dislocations we would have to endure in order to achieve Beigia-like Nirvana. As Bill Clinton well knows, we vastly prefer the *idea* of change to the reality of working to achieve it. But at least for me, the resistance runs much deeper. My discomfort with the Beigian experiment begins with the very first step—the altering of physical appearance. The Beigian solution makes me realize that I am not all that keen on living in a monochromatic world. How ironic, given the fact that if Jill and I had had children they would have contributed to the de facto Beigification of America. Even so, I would not want to live in a world in which all birds looked like starlings, or even like cardinals. Moreover, my preference for the human rainbow is not solely aesthetic. It stems from the fact that I tend to associate color difference with cultural heterogeneity. Even though ethnicity rather than race is the primary bearer of culture in our society, I have a sneaking suspicion that the more visibly distinct an ethnic group is, the more resistant it is likely to be to the homogenizing pull of American mass culture.

I have an even bigger problem when we reach step two of the Beigian solution—wiping out all memory of each inhabitant's racial identity. That move is key to ensuring an end to racism, discrimination, and bigotry. However, when we are stripped of our past, whether noble or ignoble, painful or pleasurable, we cease to exist. That is because an essential part of being who we are today is having witnessed all that we have been before.[1] If we have no memory of our yesterdays, we can't know what to make of our todays.

Imagine, for example, a mother who can no longer remember giving birth to her daughter, nurturing her, surviving the terrible twos, preparing her daughter for school, seeing her through puberty, careening with her through adolescence, or watching her grow into womanhood. Would she still be a mother? Yes, in the strictly biological sense, and yes, she would continue to live on as "Mom" in her daughter's mind, thanks to the latter's memories of the past. But in her own mind, would she be "Mom"? What could the older woman possibly make of her relationship to the younger one? And how would she see, and make sense of, herself? Clearly she is a very different person than she was before. It is as if the old self had ceased to exist and a new and distinctly different one now inhabited her body.

On Beigia, it is as if both the mother and the daughter can no longer remember themselves in relation to one another. Race, after all, is a relationship; not exactly mother-and-daughter, but something equally interdependent. Once their memories were scrambled, Beigians of all races would have lost all memory of their relationship to each other. In a real sense, the "selves" who previously populated the planet ceased to exist. And that is what I find so scary. I appreciate that an efficient and effective way to achieve racial justice would be to get rid of the old selves that remember the old ways and to start afresh with new, less encumbered ones. However, as someone who is not ready to cede my place on this earth, I'd prefer to do it the hard way.

What, then, is the moral of the Beigia thought experiment? For me, it is this: The fact that people come in different colors is not a problem, nor are racial differences necessarily a bad thing. Indeed, they may well provide an important counterforce to mindless assimilation. What needs changing is the negative value our society places on racial difference, and its use of race as a basis for maintaining a social hierarchy. The second large lesson from Beigia is that we cannot casually toss our racial past aside. It is part of the personal history each of us uses to make sense of the world and our place in it. If we are to construct a new understanding of race, we have no choice but to build on the foundations of the old.

Let's try one more thought experiment, this one briefer than the first. Imagine the planet Proportia, which, like Beigia, is an exact duplicate of Earth. There too a miracle occurs. Instead of causing people to change appearance, it alters their life circumstances. In every county, city, town, and neighborhood in Proportia's United States, 76 percent of the residents are White, 12 percent are Black, 9 percent Latino, 3 percent Asian-American, and less than 1 percent Native

American. The same proportions hold true for every school (including private nonreligious ones), for every profession and occupation, for every workplace with at least a hundred employees, and for every job title within those workplaces. Ditto the Police Athletic League, the National Honor Society, and the Future Farmers of America. When age is controlled for and recent immigrants are excluded, there are no appreciable disparities among the races in average family income or average wealth.

Proportia is thus a land of true racial equality. Would we trade places with our Proportian counterparts? Not very likely, although some of us might be tempted by the prospect of income redistribution. But it is hard for me to believe that any of us would countenance the massive dislocation that would occur in virtually every sphere of our lives. And I am not sure that many of us would be terribly enamored of Proportia's picture-perfect integration.

The lessons of the Proportia experiment are these: As we engage in the struggle to transform American race relations, we need to allow some room for freedom of choice. We also need to allow room for group characteristics and preferences to form. Suppose it turned out that in a nonhierarchical world of unrestricted opportunity Korean-Americans really did get off on and excel at math and science. Would we want to limit the percentage of such jobs they could hold? In addition, in attempting to level the playing field we should take care not to be unnecessarily disruptive. Finally, even for fire breathers like me, there may be a limit to how much we would do to achieve perfect racial justice.

Let me return, then, to the questions posed at the outset.

In my version of the Promised Land, I would not eliminate race, but I would eliminate the pecking order to which it is so closely tied. I have no idea what meaning, if any, race would acquire once it was detached from issues of privilege and power. That is rather like asking whether men would still be from Mars and women from Venus if gender hierarchy were eliminated.[2] But for now at least, I would be happy to just let it evolve. I would also take steps to undo at least some of the continuing effects of historical racial privileging, in part to level the playing field and in part to reduce the likelihood that the pecking order would simply reassert itself. In the absence of a racial hierarchy, I would not be bothered by the existence of predominantly White, partially Asian-American symphony orchestras. I'd be perfectly happy to have the NBA remain predominantly Black (though if there are any more John Stocktons or Dan Majerles out there, bring 'em on) and the NHL close to lily white. And I certainly wouldn't want every neighborhood, schoolroom, and workplace in America to resemble a racial and ethnic Noah's Ark. On the other hand, the composition of the Senate would have to change dramatically. If it did not do so through the normal electoral process, I would question seriously whether we had succeeded in uncoupling race and power.

Which brings us to the heart of the matter: How *do* we uncouple race and power? How do we dismantle the pecking order? Let me begin by saying that I share Derrick Bell's conviction that racial progress for Blacks (and, I would add, for other people of color) is achieved only when Whites view it as serving their own interests as well.[3] So it all boils down to whether it is in White people's perceived interest to dismantle the pecking order.

Putting the question of perception to the side for a moment, I do believe that racial justice *is* in White people's self-interest. People of color are not alone in suffering psychically from the racial status quo. White folk expend enormous amounts of energy justifying the awkward persistence of racial disparities in America, hiding from the reality of White skin privilege, and masking even from themselves the ways in which it operates. For over two hundred years we have struggled with the contradiction between our nation's commitment to true equality and the reality of racial stratification.[4] It would be a great relief for all concerned to resolve that contradiction in favor of our national ideals.

Less loftily, it is fast becoming evident that attitudes and practices that inhibit a large chunk of the population from fulfilling its potential are a luxury this country can no longer afford. If America is to maintain its exalted position in a highly competitive world economy, she will need to unshackle all of her citizens. Even less loftily, given the fact that in little more than a generation Whites will likely become a racial minority in America, they would be well advised to firmly establish, in practice as well as theory, the principle that systematically disadvantaging people on the basis of race is illegitimate.

It is one thing for me to believe this. It is quite another for White Americans across the board to embrace the notion that dismantling racial hierarchy is in their best interest. Perhaps it is the Pollyanna in me, or simply the part that needs a shore in sight, but I genuinely believe that this too is possible. White folk *can* see the light. But first they must work through their fears about what a brave new world would actually feel like and be like. When they are consumed by fear or paralyzed by uncertainty, people often do not do what is good for them. Ask anyone who is stuck in a relationship that she knows isn't working for her. So even granting that there are rewards aplenty to be gained from transforming race relations, a huge question remains: If we go that way, what will our lives be like? Will it be like living on Beigia or Proportia or some other strange planet?

The key to taming fear and reducing uncertainty is for all of us to find ways to actually experience racial equality firsthand. Today, before we reach the Promised Land. That has always been possible to accomplish on a micro level, even in the midst of broadscale *in*equality. After all, oppression is rarely monolithic or total. And now, more than ever, opportunities exist for White people to deal with Blacks (and other people of color) as true peers; to, in effect, try equality on for size.

Indeed the very process of racial engagement puts us all on the same plane. When we are open and honest with each other; when we abandon our hiding places, take risks, and own up to our own self-interest, when we place on the table our assumptions, fears, trepidations, and secret desires, *by that very act* we are connecting with one another as equals. For we do not, as a rule, make ourselves truly vulnerable to people we think are beneath us or beyond us. Of course, verbal engagement is just the start. For White folk to truly come to appreciate the stake they have in racial equality, they must actually experience it in their lives.

I mean more than just working, living, or even worshipping in an integrated setting. For being together in the same place and time does not necessarily mean that people are interacting on terms of true equality. More often than not, integration occurs exclusively on White people's terms. It consists of people of color being allowed to participate in a culture, an undertaking, or an environment from which they previously were, or felt, excluded. At best they are the new kids on the block, dependent on Whites for guidance, support, and even approval. Too often, there is a missionary quality to the relationship, as Whites "groom" people of color (there's an interesting word) to take over more responsible positions in time. Someday. Even when Whites and people of color are peers, there is often a significant difference in their comfort level, sense of security, and sense of belonging. Frequently the new kids feel out of their element, especially if they are having to perform on unfamiliar terrain or in a language in which they feel less than comfortable. And constrained. They feel forever on probation, and under enormous pressure to mimic the behavior and attitudes of their White colleagues.

So even in environments that look inviting on the surface, it is important to look past appearances and determine whether an invisible hierarchy is in place. The most promising settings for genuinely egalitarian interaction are ones where White folk are out of their element, where the pecking order is reversed, or where the natives get to bring religion to the missionaries instead of the other way around. Unfortunately, such settings are altogether too rare. Not surprisingly, Whites who find themselves in such settings often have difficulty adjusting to not being on top. But that, of course, is part of the lesson to be learned, for in a world in which race and power are unhinged, power will have to be shared.

Perhaps the most notable negative example is the demise of the old civil rights coalition. From the moment that Black folk insisted on assuming leadership positions, many if not most White folk headed for the hills. The reasons were, of course, several and complex. No doubt some of those who rose to power let it go to their heads, producing dissatisfaction up and down the ranks. And with the leadership shift came shifts in policy and tone, which were not to everyone's liking. Some White members were escorted to the movement's border. But most headed there under their own steam and of their own accord. The loss did have its bright side, as the women's liberation and environmental movements gained a needed infusion of activists. As Andrew Hacker has noted, in addition to being a worthy cause, "working on behalf of flora and fauna brings an additional satisfaction. These beneficiaries never grumble, or turn resentful or ungrateful. Nor is it likely that dolphins will present themselves one day and proclaim that they wish to assume control of their own struggle."[5]

Let me offer a more positive example. It is, as you might already have guessed, the Salt and Pepper Gospel Singers. Salt and Pepper is a rare example of integregation, African-American style. The music itself, its rhythms, themes, harmonies, and beat; the way we learn it, by ear rather than by sight; the way we perform it, in the clapping, swaying gospel tradition; the way rehearsals are conducted, with an emphasis on spontaneity and with ample room for the Spirit to weave in, around, and among us; and the focus on a personal rather than distant God—all this is straight out of the African-American religious tradition.

Some or all of these elements were foreign to almost all of the Salts before they joined the choir (and to some of the Peppers too, if truth be told). In recent years, Mae Gibson Brown, our founder and guiding spirit, has tried to prepare new members for the culture shock, but I'm afraid there just is no way. Folk still look as if they are ready to bolt for the door the first time they see someone talk in tongues. On the other hand, it takes remarkably little time for new Salts to settle in as if they were born to the breed.

At some level, all of us, including those who don't think of themselves as particularly religious, joined Salt and Pepper to further its ministry—spreading the good news of Jesus Christ. But for each of us, the choir holds other attractions as well. Most of the Black members have sung for years in all-Black gospel choirs, and many continue to do so in addition to hanging out with us. For them, Salt and Pepper provides a unique opportunity to interact with Whites from the high ground. There is something almost magical about getting to be ourselves and being respected at the same time. The choir is also home to a few Black folk who did not grow up in a mainstream Black church. For them, it provides a comfortable way to fill in a missing piece of our common culture. I fall somewhere in between, having been "raised up" in the Black church but having not worshipped there in a good long time. I especially love the opportunity to interact with other Black folk who take their own culture seriously, yet are secure enough to share it.

The White members joined the choir for a similar mix of reasons, but I'm confident that two are universal. Every Salty member is powerfully drawn to gospel music and to the powerful spirituality that it captures and projects. And unlike us Peppers, they don't have a lot of other options if they want to sing gospel well. The other common pull is the opportunity to interact with Black people on a genuinely human level.

We have sung in all kinds of venues, from Lincoln Center to the Apollo Theatre, from Provincetown, Massachusetts, to Charleston, South Carolina. On the very same Sunday we are apt to find ourselves in a prison in the morning and in a tony horse-country church in the evening, with an inner-city engagement in between. I couldn't possibly capture the full variety of responses we provoke, but some general patterns emerge. Black church audiences tend to receive us with exaggerated politeness at first. Their expectations are quite low, based on the assumption that White folk can't sing gospel and the even deeper assumption that they wouldn't really want to anyway. However, once they discover that we are for real and that our White members have joyfully and respectfully embraced the African-American tradition, Black audiences are wonderfully responsive and give back tremendous energy.

In contrast, predominantly White audiences are often not very demonstrative. We have learned, however, not to read too much into appearances. Often White people simply don't know how to act, or are so imbued with what they regard as proper church behavior that they can't let themselves go. Fairly regularly, people who displayed not a hint of emotion during the service or concert come up to us afterward in tears and tell us how moved they were. I recall in particular one sweet old man who described how hard it had been for him to resist the temptation to stand up and shout. We assured him that not every temptation is a sin, and suggested that he might prefer to start out slowly by patting his feet and waving his hand. Whether or not they can get into the music, White audiences seem to be moved by what they see in front of them. In many ways Salt and Pepper is a living tableau that answers Rodney King's haunting question: "Can't we all just get along?"

When I first joined the choir in 1987, its Black and

White members did not, for the most part, know very much about each other's personal lives. There were lots of preexisting friendships, but they did not tend to cross the color line. And that was fine. It was enough that we shared a common ministry in song. I suspect that many of us were a little afraid of peering into each other's lives. Certainly I was reluctant, despite my penchant for snooping. I was concerned that the more aware we became of the vast differences in our backgrounds and life circumstances—some of us were worried about whether our kids would be admitted to the graduate school of their choice while others were anxiously awaiting their kids' release from jail—the less able we would be to truly come together.

In the years since, much has changed. We have logged a lot of miles together in Salt and Pepper's decade of existence. We have boarded a lot of buses. Little by little, in twos and threes and fours, people have unfolded their lives to each other. As it turns out, the range of life situations is as broad as I imagined, though I was wrong in suspecting that White members would be massed at one end of the spectrum (any spectrum) and Black members at the other. Some very special cross-racial friendships have formed, among people whose backgrounds vary widely. But there is remarkably little pressure to "integrate." It almost seems beside the point. We do come together outside the choir from time to time, but not often. Two or three times a year we throw ourselves a party, or an individual member does the honors. And every few months, it seems, we gather as an extended family, to witness the special moments in a choir member's life, or to mourn when one of us loses a loved one.

We rarely talk as a group, except to discuss future en-

gagements or to debrief after an especially inspiring one. But
there is a moment at the end of each rehearsal, as we are
holding hands and easing into our closing prayer, when people
freely speak about life's joys and tribulations. As the Spirit
moves them, individuals ask that we pray for friends, family,
co-workers, or themselves. The prayer requests are often quite
specific: for help in finding a job; for patience in dealing with
a particular family problem; for relief from bodily pain. Members offer victory reports as well. Invariably, the news that the
operation was successful, the mortgage came through, or
Johnny made it back from California safe and sound is met
with heartfelt and occasionally boisterous thanksgiving. In
those moments, in the very act of expressing our individual
sorrows and triumphs we also testify to our common humanity.

Yet the curious thing about the Salt and Pepper Gospel
Singers is that our common humanity is rooted in an explicit
recognition of race. Our racial differences are right there in
the name. True, the reference to race is indirect, playful,
whimsical, but it is also unmistakable, especially once you see
the choir. The puckishness of the name informs one and all
that dealing with race needn't be like going to an old-fashioned dentist. Within the choir, when referring to the race of
a member or potential member we tend to rely on spice
names, as in "I was chatting with some of the Salts after
rehearsal last week." On the other hand, when referring to
race outside the choir, we seem perfectly comfortable using
Black and White. My guess is that the internal use of Salt and
Pepper allows us to affirm the primacy of choir membership
over societal definitions of race, and at the same time allows us

to maintain views about Blacks or Whites as a whole without necessarily implicating our fellow singers.

Despite the fact that Black/White racial diversity is central to our sense of who we are as a group and is explicitly acknowledged in our name, the choir has had surprising difficulty figuring out how to maintain our racial balance. Recently, for a variety of reasons, the choir began to become increasingly Salty. This disturbed me greatly, though for some reason I mostly kept my feelings to myself. But when Sheila, the original Salt, expressed the same concern to me, I almost shrieked in delight. She thanked me and said she had begun to wonder if she was crazy for thinking that the tilt was a problem, since most of the people she had spoken to wanted to leave the issue alone. And there was no easy way to air it as a group since most of us would prefer to sing than gab, especially about a topic that might produce friction and division.

One day, disturbed by the continued Whiteward drift and frustrated by our seeming inability to focus on the problem, Sheila, in her capacity as co-business manager, announced a new choir policy. Henceforth, until our balance reached fifty-fifty, we would institute a moratorium on the acceptance of new Salts and would make a concerted effort to recruit new Peppers. She acknowledged that she was being high-handed and peremptory, but expressed the view that something had to be done. Sheila's bold move certainly stirred the pot. There was no way that any of us could duck the issue any longer. The new policy spurred a good deal of conversation, and we were forced for the first time in our existence to grapple with something that made us uncomfortable.

As we discussed how intentional to be about race, Salts

and Peppers lined up on both sides of the issue. Everybody
recognized that the choir would be a very different organism if
its composition were tilted decidedly in one direction or the
other, but many were reluctant to take affirmative action to
maintain our balance. Some spoke passionately of the color-
blind ideal. If we wanted to build a world in which race no
longer mattered, they said, then we shouldn't take race into
account either. (As I listened, I wondered how they would
explain the choir's occasional practice of arranging itself in a
checkerboard pattern for concerts.) Other members felt that it
was appropriate to make special efforts to recruit new Peppers,
but that it was wrong to limit who could join. Still others
took comfort in the fact that the proposed moratorium was for
a limited period of time, until we reached a specified goal.

My guess is that for some of the Peppers who blanched
at the idea of the moratorium, their own experiences of racial
exclusion made the idea of singling out folk based on race
especially troublesome. They were so committed to not "emu-
lating the master" once they were in charge that they had
difficulty envisioning a benign use of race. I also suspect that
among the Salts were a few who just couldn't accept the idea
that there might be something from which they could be
excluded. The utter unthinkability of not being welcome anywhere and everywhere is, of course, one of the hallmarks of
White skin privilege.

Ultimately Sheila prevailed, to the choir's great benefit.
The only significant change was that the moratorium was limited in time. We became much more purposeful in our re-
cruitment of new members, and much more concerned that
they received a genuinely warm welcome. The entire experi-

ence forced us to think more carefully about who we want to be and what we want to represent. And it revealed to us that we have the power to shape ourselves in the image we desire. It was also quite humbling. We had grown rather smug regarding our ability to deal with race. But we discovered that, like anyone else, we have difficulty dealing with difficult things. And sometimes we prefer comfort to stirring the pot, even when we know it needs it.

Is Salt and Pepper the Promised Land? In many ways yes, but it is an awfully tiny land indeed. The choir is, of course, a work-in-progress, as is every human endeavor. Yet certain features seem fixed. We have not run away from race or tried to make it go away. In fact, we have placed it front and center. And in that very act we have created the possibility of altering its meaning. Within the choir, race is linked with life experiences, history, culture, and modes of presentation, but it is not linked with power. A soprano is a soprano is a soprano. We recognize that Blacks' voices tend to differ from those of Whites in timbre and character, so we have made a conscious effort to blend them. But we have not blended the basic style of Black gospel music. Integration has not meant homogenization.

The same is true on a personal level. Although it is fair to say that each and every member of Salt and Pepper has been transformed by the experience of performing with the choir, in important respects we also remain the same people we were when we joined. No one has changed color. No one has changed race. No one's culture has been lost or sacrificed. We have managed to blend and be respectful of difference at the same time. The only thing we have given up is the right to dominate one another. No one's history has been altered. But together we have the power to transform the future.

That is my vision of the Promised Land. It is not grand, but it is real. And it is attainable. All it takes is a genuine commitment to the process of racial healing.

Notes

INTRODUCTION

1. I borrow the simile from Wendell Berry's thoughtful meditation on race. Wendell Berry, *The Hidden Wound* (Boston: Houghton Mifflin, 1970).

2. See Jeannye Thornton, David Whitman, and Dorian Friedman, "White's Myths About Blacks," *U.S. News and World Report,* 9 November 1992, 41, 43; Harris Poll conducted 21 October 1991; Gallup Poll conducted August 1993, sponsored by CNN and *USA Today,* available from Roper Center for Public Opinion Research, University of Connecticut; National Opinion Research Center General Social Survey 1993, available from Roper Center; Joint Center for Political Studies survey conducted September 1988. Not surprisingly, numerous Whites oppose programs that attempt to assist Blacks and make up for past inequalities. See NBC News/*Wall Street Journal* poll conducted June 1993 by Hart and Teeter Research Company, available from Roper Center; Philip Bennett and Victoria Benning, "Racial Lines Recast by New Generation: Greater Interaction Has Failed to Span Divide," *Boston Globe,* 13 September 1992.

3. See, for example, Peter Kihss, " 'Benign Neglect' on Race is Proposed by Moynihan," *New York Times,* 1 March 1970; Anthony Lewis,

"Neglect—Benign or Hostile?" *New York Times*, 2 March 1970; Editorial, "Neglect—but Not 'Benign,' " *New York Times*, 3 March 1970; Linda Charlton, "21 Rights Leaders Rebut Moynihan: Assert 'Benign Neglect' Idea is 'Symptomatic of Effort to Wipe Out Gains,' " *New York Times*, 6 March 1970; Roy Wilkins, "Not So Benign," *New York Post*, 14 March 1970.

II. HEALING THE PAST/TRANSFORMING THE PRESENT
Engagement

1. David T. Wellman, *Portraits of White Racism*, 2d ed. (New York: Cambridge University Press, 1993), 179–80, 185.

2. Jean Genet, *The Thief's Journal* (New York: Grove Press, Inc. 1964), 176.

3. *Blank v. Sullivan & Cromwell*, 418 F Supp 1, 4 (SDNY 1975).

4. Wellman, *White Racism*, 201.

5. Woody Allen, *Annie Hall* (1977), feature-length film.

6. Wellman, *White Racism*, 175.

7. Jill Nelson, review of *Colored People: A Memoir*, by Henry Louis Gates, Jr., *Nation*, 6 June 1994, 794.

8. Jacqueline Adams, "The White Wife," *New York Times*, 18 September 1994.

Race

1. Cornel West easily wins the prize for the most brilliant and simultaneously serviceable book title of the decade. Cornel West, *Race Matters* (Boston: Beacon Press, 1993).

2. Office of Management and Budget, *Directive No. 15, Race and Ethnic Standards for Federal Statistics and Administrative Reporting*, notice published in the *Federal Register* (Washington, D.C., May 4, 1978), 19269–70.

3. Laura Gomez, "A Multidimensional Typology of 'Race': A Preliminary Application in the Jury Selection Context" (paper presented at the annual meeting of the Association of American Law Schools, New Orleans, La., January 1995); *Idem*, "The Birth of the 'Hispanic' Genera-

tion: Attitudes of Mexican-American Political Elites Toward the Hispanic Label," *Latin American Perspectives* 19, no. 4 (Fall 1992): 45–58.

4. Lawrence Wright, "One Drop of Blood," *The New Yorker*, 25 July 1994, 47.

5. Shirley Taylor Haizlip, "Passing," *American Heritage*, February/March 1995, 47–48.

6. Adrian Piper, "Passing for White, Passing for Black," *Transition* 58 (1992): 4.

7. Shirley Taylor Haizlip, *The Sweeter the Juice* (New York: Touchstone, 1994), 241–68.

8. Rodolfo Acuna, *Occupied America: A History of Chicanos,* 3rd ed. (New York: Harper & Row, 1988), 55–56.

9. See generally Samuel Betances, "African-Americans and Hispanics/ Latinos: Eliminating Barriers to Coalition Building," in *The State of Black Hartford,* ed. Stanley Battle (Hartford: The Urban League of Greater Hartford, Inc., 1993); Betances, "The Prejudice of Having No Prejudice in Puerto Rico," *The Rican* (Winter 1972): 41–54; Frank F. Montalvo, *The Origins and Contemporary Patterns of Ethnoracial Ambiguity Among Mexican Americans and Puerto Ricans* (San Antonio: Our Lady of the Lake University of San Antonio, 1987); Melita Marie Garza, "Black Hispanics Taking Pride in Their Multifaceted Heritage," *Chicago Tribune,* 16 September 1992.

10. See, for example, Lynn Norment, "Who's Black and Who's Not?: New Ethnicity Raises Provocative Questions About Racial Identity," *Ebony,* March 1990, 134–39.

11. See Lynn Norment, "Mariah Carey: Singer Talks About Storybook Marriage, Interracial Heritage, and Sudden Fame," *Ebony,* April 1994, 54–60; Idem, "Mariah Carey: 'Not Another White Girl Trying to Sing Black," *Ebony,* March 1991, 54–58.

12. See, for example, Lynn Norment, "The Many Talents of Paula Abdul: Sassy Entertainer Gives Expanded Definition to Term 'Multiple,' " *Ebony,* May 1990, 118–22.

13. For dialogue regarding "Who's Black and Who's Not?" see Letters to the Editor, *Ebony,* May 1990, 12–15; Letters to the Editor, *Ebony,* June 1990, 148, 150, 152. Responses regarding Mariah Carey are included in Letters to the Editor, *Ebony,* May 1991, 16, 18; Letters to the

Editor, *Ebony,* June 1994, 8; Letters to the Editor, *Ebony,* July 1994, 11–12.

14. Alex Jones, " 'Geraldo' Gambles on Talk," *New York Times,* 6 September 1987.

15. "Treason to Whiteness Is Loyalty to Humanity: An Interview with Noel Ignatiev of Race Traitor Magazine," *Utne Reader,* no. 66 (November/December 1994): 82–86.

16. Wellman, *White Racism,* 4.

Healing

1. Berry, *The Hidden Wound.*
2. John W. Blassingame, *Frederick Douglass: The Clarion Voice* (Division of Publications, National Park Service, United States Department of the Interior, 1976), 46.
3. Tony Paterson, "Mengele Victim Recalls 'Nights of Terror,' " *United Press International,* 26 January 1985; Alice Siegert, "President of Israel Begins German Visit: Herzog Returns to Death Camp Site," *Chicago Tribune,* 7 April 1987.
4. Judith Miller, *One, by One, by One* (New York: Simon & Schuster, 1990), 13–32; Greer Fay Cashman, "The Hard Road Back to the Warsaw Ghetto," *Jerusalem Post,* 11 April 1991.
5. Langston Hughes, *Lenox Avenue Mural,* in *American Negro Poetry,* ed. Arna Bontemps (New York: Hill and Wang, 1963), 67–68.

III. WHAT WHITE FOLK MUST DO
White Skin Privilege

1. Wellman, *White Racism,* 194–95.
2. Ibid., 136–37, 163, 186–87.
3. Peggy McIntosh, "White Privilege: Unpacking the Invisible Knapsack," *Peace and Freedom,* July/August 1989, 10.
4. Ibid., 10–11.
5. Wellman, *White Racism,* 136–37.
6. McIntosh, "White Privilege," 10.
7. Ibid., 11.

Owning

1. See generally Wellman, *White Racism,* for a discussion of White peoples' thinking in this regard.
2. Michele Galen and Ann Therese Palmer, "White, Male, and Worried," *Business Week,* 31 January 1994, 50–55.
3. "White Male Fear," *Economist,* 29 January 1994, 34.
4. Warren Farrell, "The Myth of Male Power," parts 1 and 2, *Playboy,* July 1993, August 1993.
5. David Gates, "White Male Paranoia," *Newsweek,* 29 March 1993, 48–53.
6. J. Hoberman, "Victim Victorious: Well-Fed Yuppie Michael Douglas Leads the Charge for Resentful White Men," *Village Voice,* 7 March 1995, 31–33; "Tapping Male Fears: Michael Douglas Finds Success as 'Victim,' " *Cleveland Plain Dealer,* 31 December 1994; Ellen Goodman, " 'Disclosure' Uncovers Hollywood Distortion," *Chicago Tribune,* 20 December 1994.
7. See generally Robert C. Smith and Richard Seltzer, *Race, Class, and Culture: A Study in Afro-American Mass Opinion* (Albany: State University of New York Press, 1992), chapter one.
8. Ellis Cose, *The Rage of a Privileged Class* (New York: HarperCollins, 1993).
9. Wellman, *White Racism,* 112.

Horatio Alger

1. Edwin P. Hoyt, *Horatio's Boys: The Life and Works of Horatio Alger, Jr.* (Radnor, Penn.: Chilton Book Company, 1974).
2. Stephen L. Carter, *Reflections of an Affirmative Action Baby* (New York: Basic Books, 1991), 47–49.
3. Sandy Grady, "Will He or Won't He?: Win or Lose, Presidential Pursuit by Colin Powell Would Do America a Necessary Service," *Kansas City Star,* 24 April 1995; Thomas B. Edsall, "For Powell, Timing Could be Crucial: As Gulf War Hero Hints at 1996 Bid, Associates Look into Details," *Washington Post,* 6 April 1995; J. F. O. McAllister,

"The Candidate of Dreams," *Time,* 13 March 1995; Deroy Murdock, "Colin Powell: Many Things to Many People," *Washington Times,* 16 January 1995; Doug Fischer, "U.S. Politics: War Hero Well-Placed to Become First Black President," *Ottawa Citizen,* 8 October 1994; "General Nice Guy: Profile Colin Powell," *Sunday Telegraph,* 25 September 1994; Otto Kreisher, "As a Civilian, Powell's Options are Enviable," *San Diego Union-Tribune,* 26 September 1993.

4. Shelley E. Taylor, *Positive Illusions: Creative Self-Deception and the Healthy Mind* (New York: Basic Books, 1989), xi.

5. Ibid., xi, 7, 228–46.

6. Ibid., xi.

7. Robert T. Carter, et al., "White Racial Identity Development and Work Values," *Journal of Vocational Behavior, Special Issue: Racial Identity and Vocational Behavior* 44, no. 2 (April 1994): 185–97.

Resisting Temptation

1. Ronald Takaki, *Strangers from a Different Shore: A History of Asian-Americans* (New York: Penguin Books, 1989), 475–76.

2. Ann Scott Tyson, "Asian-Americans Spurn Image as Model Minority," *Christian Science Monitor,* 26 August 1994. A recent study of Los Angeles County called "Beyond Asian-American Poverty" also concluded that substantial numbers of Asian-Americans lack the job and language skills needed to rise out of poverty. Despite working full-time, many Asian-Americans continue to live in poverty. K. Connie Kang, "Study Finds Neglect of Asian Poor; Communities: Poverty Rate in County is Twice That of Whites, UCLA Researchers Say; Report Cites 'Model Minority' Image as Reason Why Many in Need are Overlooked by Government Policy Makers," *Los Angeles Times,* 2 December 1993.

3. Sumi K. Cho, "Model Minority Mythology in Antidiscrimination Law: The Foundation of the Strict Scrutiny Review in Affirmative Action," (unpublished manuscript on file with the author); Takaki, *Strangers from a Different Shore,* 475.

4. Sucheng Chan, *Asian-Americans: An Interpretive History* (Boston: Twayne, 1991), 168.

5. "A Reluctant Jackson," segment by Charlayne Hunter-Gault, *Mac-Neil/Lehrer News Hour,* Public Broadcasting System, 11 July 1984; David Bird, "Mondale Denounces Muslim Remark on Judaism," *New York Times,* 27 June 1984; Howell Raines, "Rivals in Debate Criticize Jackson on Backer's Acts," *New York Times,* 3 May 1984; David S. Broder, "Mondale Predicts 'Surprise' for Reagan at Polls; Candidate Assails Farrakhan Remarks," *Washington Post,* 24 April 1984.

6. Joseph Berger, "Jewish Leaders Criticize Jackson; The Democrats Are Also Warned," *New York Times,* 11 July 1984; Phil Gailey, "Democrats Hail Jackson Shift on Muslim, but Fears Persist," *New York Times,* 30 June 1984; "Campaign Notes; Party Will Not Disavow Jackson, Chairman Says," *New York Times,* 4 June 1984.

7. "Senate Judiciary Committee Confirmation Hearing of Deval Patrick to Be Assistant Attorney General for Civil Rights," *Federal News Service,* 10 March 1994; Karen Hosler and Lyle Denniston, "Black Caucus Backs Civil Rights Nominee," *Baltimore Sun,* 11 February 1994; Clint Bolick and Elaine Jones, interview by James Lehrer, *MacNeil/Lehrer News Hour,* Public Broadcasting System, 1 February 1994.

8. Neil A. Lewis, "Senate Democrats Urge Withdrawal of Rights Nominee," *New York Times,* 2 June 1993; Michael Isikoff, "Confirmation Battle Looms Over Guinier: Critics Target 'Extreme' Views in Law Review Articles by Justice Department Civil Rights Nominee," *Washington Post,* 21 May 1993.

IV. WHAT BLACK FOLK MUST DO
Retell the Story

1. Ken Hamblin, "Speaking Well Has Its Merits," *Denver Post,* 28 March 1995; David Grogan, "The Avenger: Ken Hamblin, Whom Critics Call the Black Rush Limbaugh, Baits Liberals and Hooks Listeners," *Time,* 12 December 1994, 105; Ken Hamblin, interview by Bob Herbert, in "Who Will Help the Black Man?" symposium moderated by Bob Herbert, *New York Times,* 4 December 1994.

2. "No More Excuses," segment by Catherine Crier with comments of Stanley Crouch, Darryl Mobley, Star Parker, Errol Smith, and Walter Williams, *20/20,* American Broadcasting Companies, 13 May 1994;

Stanley Crouch, James A. Forbes, Jr., Donald L. Sharp, and Robert Woodson, interview by Robert MacNeil, *MacNeil/Lehrer News Hour,* Public Broadcasting System, 15 November 1993.

3. Alan M. Dershowitz, *The Abuse Excuse: Cop-outs, Sob Stories, and Other Evasions of Responsibility* (Boston: Little, Brown, 1994).

4. William Styron, *The Confessions of Nat Turner* (New York: Random House, 1967).

5. William Styron, "Slavery's Pain, Disney's Gain," *New York Times,* 4 August 1994.

6. Ibid.

7. Ibid.

8. D. Marvin Jones, "Darkness Made Visible: Law, Metaphor, and the Racial Self," 82 *Georgetown Law Journal* 437, 459 (1993). I owe Professor Jones credit for most of the ideas in this paragraph and the next.

9. "Reporter's Notebook; Baton is 'Star' in Police-Beating Trial," *New York Times,* 6 April 1992. See generally Sheri Lynn Johnson, "Racial Imagery in Criminal Cases," 67 *Tulane Law Review* 1739 (1993).

10. "Reporter's Notebook; Baton is 'Star.' "

11. "Anita Hill and Clarence Thomas: Public Hearing, Private Pain," documentary by Ofra Bikel, *Frontline,* Public Broadcasting System, 13 October 1992; Nellie Y. McKay, "Remembering Anita Hill and Clarence Thomas: What Really Happened When One Black Woman Spoke Out," in *Race-ing Justice, En-gendering Power,* ed. Toni Morrison (New York: Pantheon Books, 1992), 281–82; "Race Affects How Some View Tyson, O.J. Cases," *Indianapolis Star,* 27 March 1995; Barry Cooper, "Simpson Must Rely on African-American Support," *Orlando Sentinel,* 23 October 1994.

12. Harlon L. Dalton, "AIDS in Blackface," *Daedalus, Journal of the American Academy of Arts and Sciences* 118, no. 3 (Summer 1989): 205–27.

13. Ira Berkow, "The Coloring of Bird," *New York Times,* 2 June 1987.

14. Ibid.

15. Alexis de Tocqueville, *Democracy in America,* ed. J. P. Mayer (New York: Harper & Row, 1988), 535–38.

16. Joseph Marshall, interview by Bob Herbert, in "Who Will Help the Black Man?"

17. Andrew Hacker, *Two Nations: Black and White, Separate, Hostile, Unequal* (New York: Ballantine Books, 1995), 241.

18. Ibid., 103.

19. Ibid., 108–9.

20. Ibid., 101.

21. Ibid., 105–6.

22. Michael Quint, "Anti-Black Bias Still Found in Mortgage Applications," *New York Times,* 2 October 1992; *Idem,* "Making a Difference; Tracking Bias in Banks," *New York Times,* 16 February 1992; *Idem,* "Racial Gap Detailed on Mortgages," *New York Times,* 22 October 1991; *Idem,* "Mortgage Race Data Show Gap," *New York Times,* 14 October 1991.

23. See studies cited in Wellman, *White Racism,* 18–19.

24. "The B.E. 100s: Industrial/Service Companies," *Black Enterprise,* June 1994, 87–90.

25. Cose, *Privileged Class,* 32.

26. Ibid., 56–68.

27. Harlon L. Dalton, "The Clouded Prism," *Harvard Civil Rights Civil Liberties Law Review* 22, no. 2 (1987): 443.

28. For an overview of the story, see David Usborne, "Klan Turns Town Into Laughing Stock," *The Independent,* 26 September 1993.

29. Courtland Milloy, "We Have Met the Enemy . . ." *Washington Post,* 19 September 1993.

30. See Deborah Shelton Pinkney, "Why Do Some People Get Sicker than Others?" *American Medical News* 37, no. 48 (6 December 1994); David R. Williams, Risa Lavizzo-Mourey, Rueben C. Warren, "The Concept of Race and Health Status in America; Papers from the CDC-ATSDR Workshop on the Use of Race and Ethnicity in Public Health Surveillance," *Public Health Reports* 109, no. 1 (January 1994).

Pull Together as the Community

1. Regina Austin, "The Black Community, Its Lawbreakers, and a Politics of Identification," 65 *Southern California Law Review* 1769 (May 1992).

2. Martha Minow, "Stories in Law," paper presented at the Narrative

and Rhetoric in the Law conference, sponsored by Yale Law School and the Whitney Humanities Center, New Haven, Ct., 10 February 1995.

3. David J. Dent, "The New Black Suburbs," *New York Times,* 14 June 1992.

4. Ibid.

5. Carter, *Affirmative Action Baby,* 237–41.

6. Stephen Carter hints at this as well. Ibid., 241. In a somewhat different context, David Wilkins develops what he calls the "obligation thesis" to explain why successful Black lawyers should give back to the community. See David B. Wilkins, "Two Paths to the Mountaintop? The Role of Legal Education in Shaping the Values of Black Corporate Lawyers," 45 *Stanford Law Review* 1981 (July 1993).

7. Marlon Riggs, *Tongues Untied* (55 minutes, 1989), documentary.

8. Kimberle Crenshaw, "Mapping the Margins: Intersectionality, Identity Politics, and Violence Against Women of Color," 43 *Stanford Law Review* 1241, 1256–57 (July 1991).

9. Ibid., 1273–75.

10. See McKay, "Remembering Anita Hill and Clarence Thomas," in Morrison, *Race-ing Justice,* 273–75; Margaret A. Burnham, "The Supreme Court Appointment Process and the Politics of Race and Sex," in Morrison, *Race-ing Justice,* 307–15; documentary, "Public Hearing, Private Pain."

11. Bert James Loewenberg and Ruth Bogin, eds., *Black Women in Nineteenth-Century American Life* (University Park, Penn.: Pennsylvania State University Press, 1976), 235.

12. Kendall Thomas, "Strange Fruit," in Morrison, *Race-ing Justice,* 370–71.

13. Nell Irwin Paitner, "Hill, Thomas, and the Use of Racial Stereotype," in Morrison, *Race-ing Justice,* 209–13.

Take Stock of Our Culture

1. Zach Dunkin, "Swearing by 'the N word,' " *Indianapolis News,* 30 September 1994.

2. Ibid.

3. John Freeman, " 'Gangsta Rap' Comes Under Fire; Many Radio

Stations Banning It, but Sales Still Soar," *San Diego Union-Tribune,* 17 December 1993; David Usborne, "Wiggers Just Wannabe Black; White Middle-Class Kids Are Adopting Black Street Style and Chilling Out to Rap Music," *Independent,* 22 August 1993.

4. Esther Iverem, "Pointing Fingers: Blacks Vocally Disagree About Prevalent Current Images," *St. Louis Post-Dispatch,* 7 November 1993; Rick Kogan, "HBO Spreads a Gritty 'Jam'; Comedy Show Serves Its Laughs with a Big Helping of Reality," *Chicago Tribune,* 26 August 1993.

5. See, for example, Richard Roeper, "Nothing's Changed at N. Newton High," *Chicago Sun-Times,* 3 April 1994; Darlene Himmelspach, "Student Calls Hate-Crime Allegation Absurd," *San Diego Union-Tribune,* 9 April 1994; "What Is a Wigger?" transcript of *The Oprah Winfrey Show,* 9 September 1993; transcript of *The Today Show,* 18 August 1993.

6. For an extraordinary portrait of the economic, cultural, and spiritual decline of predominantly White, blue-collar Lakewood, California, "once the ideal postwar town . . . [now] best known as the home of the Spur Posse, a gang of high-school athletes who counted their sexual conquests as 'points' in what may be the only game left in town," see Joan Didion, "Letter from California: Trouble in Lakewood," *The New Yorker,* 26 July 1993, 46–65.

7. Havelock Nelson, "New Campaign to Crush 'Negative' Rap," *Billboard,* 22 May 1993; Reverend Dr. Calvin O. Butts, III, "Rolling Out an Agenda for Rap," *Billboard,* 19 June 1993.

8. Esther Iverem, "Negative Black Stereotypes Abound in Rap Lyrics, on Music Videos, in Movies, and on Cable—and Blacks Are Among Those Doing the Stereotyping," *Newsday,* 24 October 1993; Butts, "Rolling Out an Agenda."

9. Ann Scales, "Rap-Lyric Initiative Draws Favorable Response," *Dallas Morning News,* 5 August 1993.

10. Ibid.

11. Ibid.

12. See, for example, Brent Staples, "Editorial Notebook: The Politics of Gangster Rap," *New York Times,* 27 August 1993.

13. Butts, "Rolling Out an Agenda."

NOTES

Welcome the New Kids on the Block

1. See generally Robert N. Clinton, "Redressing the Legacy of Conquest: A Vision Quest for a Decolonized Federal Indian Law," 46 *Arkansas Law Review* 77 (1993).
2. See Neil Gotanda, "Asian-American Rights and the 'Miss Saigon Syndrome,' " in *Asian-Americans and the Supreme Court,* ed., Hyung-chan Kim (New York: Greenwood Press, 1992), 1087–98; Gotanda, "Other Non-Whites" in *"American Legal History: A Review of Justice at War,"* 85 *Columbia Law Review* 1186, 1188 (1985).

V. THE PROMISED LAND

1. I owe this insight to Stephen Sarfaty. See also Padma Perera, "The Witness Within," *Parabola: The Magazine of Myth and Tradition* 11, no. 1 (February 1995): 66–73.
2. The reference, of course, is to John Gray's long-time best seller *Men Are from Mars, Women Are from Venus* (New York: HarperCollins, 1992).
3. See Derrick Bell, "Brown and the Interest-Convergence Dilemma," in *Shades of Brown: New Perspectives on School Desegregation,* ed. Derrick Bell (New York: Teachers College, Columbia University, 1980), 91–106.
4. See Derrick Bell, *Faces at the Bottom of the Well: The Permanence of Racism* (New York: Basic Books, 1992).
5. Hacker, *Two Nations,* 70.